The Readers' Advisory Guide to
Graphic Novels

ALA READERS' ADVISORY SERIES

The Readers' Advisory Guide to
Graphic Novels

Francisca Goldsmith

American Library Association

Chicago   2010

Francisca Goldsmith has been working with readers, potential readers, and graphic novels in libraries for more than twenty years. An active member of the Young Adult Library Services Association, she helped to facilitate ALA's first graphic-novel-focused preconference in 2002, and she organized a sequential-art-themed preconference at YALSA's first Young Adult Literature Symposium in 2008. She teaches library staff members who are becoming familiar with graphic novels through YALSA and the California Infopeople Project. She is the author of *Graphic Novels Now: Building, Managing, and Marketing a Dynamic Collection* (American Library Association, 2005). By day, she's the director of branch services of Halifax Public Libraries in Nova Scotia.

The paper used in this publication meets the minimum requirements of American National Standard for Information Sciences—Permanence of Paper for Printed Library Materials, ANSI Z39.48-1992. ∞

Library of Congress Cataloging-in-Publication Data

Goldsmith, Francisca.

The readers' advisory guide to graphic novels / Francisca Goldsmith.

p.   cm. — (ALA readers' advisory series)

Includes bibliographical references and index.

ISBN 978-0-8389-1008-5 (alk. paper)

1. Libraries—Special collections—Graphic novels. 2. Graphic novels—Bibliography. 3. Readers' advisory services—United States. I. Title.

Z692.G7G655 2010

025.2'77415—dc22   2009025239

ISBN-13: 978-0-8389-1008-5

Printed in the United States of America

14   13   12   11   10   5   4   3   2   1

CONTENTS

INTRODUCTION

The critical and professional literature available to library staff working with comics and graphic novels has grown vastly over the past decade, with a couple of new books published annually and journal articles appearing regularly year-round. The amount of discursive advice for general readers has also grown like Topsy during this time. However, the link that would bring formal readers' advisory work to bear on the format has remained ephemeral. Occasionally, suggestions on how to promote reading advice to those already reading graphic novels, and different advice about how to promote graphic novels to youth who are aliterate, appear as sidebars, brief chapters, or elements of professional presentations on graphic novels or on promoting adolescent literacy.

This book seeks to promote readers' advisory work with the format, rather than using the format as a tool to promote reading. It is not intended to be the final word on the topic, but rather an opening for that conversation. This book cannot live on its own; it requires curious and insightful advisors as well as the critical body of work already noted as accruing around graphic novels.

The conversation about how to advance the connection between readers and comics and potential readers and comics appears in need of plumbing, in part because now we can stop being defensive and start being proactive. The iron grip that seemed to be holding graphic novels in an age-specific neighborhood is loosening. Manga series aimed at teen audiences are still easy to sell, but considerably more diversity of fine alternatives is now available. And recognition that teens aren't the only graphic novel readers is beginning to dawn in professional discussions, as it already did years ago among readers themselves.

New Yorker art editor Françoise Mouly has launched Toon Books, an imprint that addresses the desire for very young children to have graphic novels appropriate to their developmental abilities as prereaders and aesthetes. First Second has demonstrated staying power as a publisher of literary graphic novels for children, teens, and now older readers too. In addition to continued health on the parts of independent publishers including Dark Horse, Drawn and Quarterly, Fantagraphics, Image Comics, NBM, Oni Press, Slave Labor Graphics, Top Shelf, and Viz, big houses continue to support comics and graphic novel publishing for adults and youth through TokyoPop, Pantheon, Hill and Wang, and Yen Press. More North American publishers are noting the appetite of readers for translations and providing more international breadth to their productions. In turn, this means readers and potential readers have more opportunity to expand their choices from American-made and translated Japanese works to graphic novels from Western and Eastern Europe, Africa, and several Asian countries.

At the library, Gene Luen Yang's Printz Award for *American Born Chinese* opened doors to graphic novels for youth even in communities where the format had been considered reading on the down low.[1] Adult collections of graphic novels were given a boost at the library in the first few years of the twenty-first century, when movie makers invested in bringing a variety to the big screen: *Ghost World, American Splendor, Sin City, 300,* and *Persepolis* are just a handful of films that show the variety and adult-friendly content of graphic novels.

Publishing on the format has been blossoming; see chapter 8 for titles by and for librarians (and lay readers) that offer comprehensive bibliographies of graphic novels. However, vastly more attention is being paid in print and in workshops to collection development than to advisory work. The readers' advisory angles that are most frequently mentioned in the literature focus on the collection first—an entity to be displayed, organized, made available—and not so much on either the reader or the advising aspects of the synthesis that includes subject, object, and action, or reader, graphic novel, and advising.

Professional advising of readers more generally has been enjoying a lengthy renaissance, with most of the attention focused on advising adults. Genre-specific advisory tools are offered in book and web format. On rarer occasions, we find format-specific advisory lists for such audiences as readers in need of large print or connections between the book and film collections. These format-specific tools are almost always simple lists, not guidance on how to talk with readers and potential readers about specific formats.

That's the niche this title is intended to address. Annotated bibliographies are essential to those who can't possibly read and remember every relevant title in a particular area. But readers' advisory work isn't about lists; it's an activity that requires one to recognize features of both readers and books and to bring about a conversation that can lead the reader to a desirable book. Readers' advisory work draws all five of S. R. Rangana-than's Laws of Library Science to bear in one activity.

How one advises must change to keep in tune as much with format as with individual readers. Advising a listener is markedly different (in some ways) from advising a visual reader of traditional print texts. The same can be said for advising about the format of graphic novels. Chapter 1 discusses the essential qualities of the format and the specific attributes of a reader engaged with a graphic novel. Chapter 2 discusses basic read-ers' advisory methods with reference to the graphic novel format as the particular context. Chapter 3 offers guidance to advisors who are working with experienced readers of graphic novels and comics, while chapter 4 provides assistance in moving readers who are unfamiliar with the format toward it. Chapter 5 discusses relationships between graphic novels and other media that can be explored and exploited by the readers' advisor. Chapters 6 and 7 offer annotated lists that can serve as suggested paths along which to move readers who seek prescribed directions. Chapter 8 collects a variety of readers' advisory tools.

If you, as a readers' advisor, are not already familiar with graphic novel reading firsthand, you should probably start with the short course available in appendix A. Otherwise, you risk placing yourself in the dis-honest position of offering advice without knowing what your advice seeker might know or feel, and you may be left without the means to refer compellingly to the graphic novels in your collection.

It took considerably longer to develop and write this book than I had imagined when I first discussed the idea for it over a beer in one of Bos-ton's tiniest bars, Bukowski's Tavern, known locally for its Dead Authors Club. And although the work certainly didn't kill me, I did lose my good friend Rory Root, of Berkeley's Comic Relief, to an untimely death, and moved thirty-eight hundred miles myself, all during the course of putting this book together. And those were just the larger stumbling blocks.

On the upside, the four years between suggesting and finishing this book have allowed me to explore readers' advisory work, libraries, the library profession, and, of course, comics in a large number of communi-ties and carry on lengthy discussions with public, school, and academic library and publishing partners about the format in general and particular instances of it in all their glory. The profusion of social networking options at my fingertips means that book discussions can now go on 24-7 and without regard to geographic distance.

Thanks, as ever, to Bob, who this time was left to pack unassisted all three thousand of our books as we moved from Berkeley to Halifax. The graphic novels filled boxes 1–6, 10, 17, and 18, according to the annotated list he prepared for customs. And that didn't take into account the ones I had accrued during my year alone here in Halifax, thanks to Strange Adventures and the kind mailings from Todd Martinez, who is keeping the light on back at Comic Relief.

What are you reading? And why should I? That's the beginning of the most casual—and essential—readers' advisory opportunity. With graphic novels, the added essential conveyed in these casual suggestions is how the narrative is put together. Where does the weight lie, in the visual or text component, or in that perfect magic place that stands on the shoulders of image and word at once? Editor and illustrator Mark Siegel describes graphic novels as presenting a dance between pictures and words.[2] That would place the readers' advisor near the punch bowl with a ladle, ready to offer refreshment and send the dancers back onto the floor.

Notes

1. Gene Luen Yang, *American Born Chinese* (New York: First Second Books, 2006).
2. Francisca Goldsmith, "Words and Pictures Dancing Together: In Conversation with Mark Siegel," *Voice of Youth Advocates* (June 2007): 124–27.

1
WHAT'S SPECIAL ABOUT GRAPHIC NOVELS
A Background for Readers' Advisors

The art of providing individuals and groups with advice on what to read next and why continues to become a refined craft for North American librarians. In professional circles, the likes of Joyce Saricks, Neal Wyatt, and Duncan Smith are recognized as leaders and innovators in this pursuit of sharing books effectively, while Nancy Pearl enjoys a reputation beyond libraryland among the very laity whom we would advise. Children's librarians, young adult librarians, school librarians, and, more recently, academic librarians are aware of the role that advising readers has to play in promoting use of the library, and also in helping communities develop increased intellectual health and civic engagement. Just as the experience of communication itself has become increasingly rapid, highly textured, and collaborative, so too has systematic reading advice become more sophisticated and ubiquitous.

If you aren't a reader, then working as a readers' advisor may be difficult. If you aren't familiar with the graphic novel format, you might want to turn to appendix A first, and spend some time with the format before moving into an advisory role with other readers and potential readers.

DO READERS NEED GRAPHIC NOVEL ADVICE?

In the course of this book, we will discuss how graphic novels can provide suitable and welcome reading material to confirmed fans, those who have not yet read comics, and many potential audience targets between those extremes.

A couple of myths about graphic novels and reading audiences have developed as the format has become increasingly accepted in North

American libraries. These two are most detrimental to developing healthy reader services to promote the reading of graphic novels:

> Myth 1: Graphic novels are a format appropriate specifically to adolescent readers.

> Myth 2: Reading graphic novels, and comics generally, can be accomplished readily by those with low or compromised literacy skills, making the format universally appropriate to poor readers and audiences new to English.

As is typically the case with myths, a grain of truth lies within each of these, but that grain has been overwhelmed by generalizing from particular circumstances to the viewpoint of truism in all circumstances.

Truths behind Myth 1

Many graphic novels are indeed appropriate to adolescent readers. Some of these are especially attractive to teens, while others are attractive and appropriate to other age groups—older *and* younger—as well as to teens. However, many graphic novels are wholly inappropriate to teen readers, being either too juvenile or too sophisticated, or concerning a topic outside the realm of awareness someone can develop before middle age or so.

The myth about teens as the target for graphic novel collecting in libraries grew from a set of developmental circumstances concerning North American public and school library service, not development of the format. While the first libraries to make concerted efforts to collect comics and graphic novels tended to be academic ones in which such materials received archival attention, the format's arrival in less hallowed grounds occurred through efforts exerted by a number of public and school librarians who happened to be working largely with young adults. Some may want to draw sociological conclusions about the apparent penchant among young adult librarians to be inclusive of the format at a time when specialist librarians serving younger and older groups were less welcoming. Whatever the reason, because of the lead taken by this particular service group, a false premise arose in many library circles that the format is specifically linked to teen reading.

Truths behind Myth 2

While the solidly printed page may indeed seem more daunting to a reader with uncertain skills than a page broken into both verbal and image languages, there is nothing innately remedial or simplified about reading graphic novels and comics. The reader must work with both visual and verbal literacies with this format; images do not illustrate or repeat verbal content, but provide information and sensibility not communicated through the text.

Many contemporary cultures have comics traditions, especially in North America, parts of Europe, and Asia. However, not all cultures have indigenous comics traditions and may be familiar only with imports of juvenilia from Disney or Belgium, or imports from Japan that are geared to specific age groups. (See appendix B.) Presenting new Americans with graphic novels as a stopgap measure on their way to gaining English reading fluency needs to be handled in a culturally respectful and informed manner. This is not a one-size-fits-all format.

Advising graphic novel readers and others for whom graphic novels may be appropriate and welcome reading material must be undertaken with cultural sensitivity, as well as an awareness of format.

How does providing advice about which graphic novels to read compare to the aspects of the advisor's art limned by the literature to date? On the one hand, a graphic novel is a book, and the reader brings a set of experiences and hopes to that book, just as the book and the reader meet in advisory situations that correspond to more traditional print formats. On the other hand, graphic novels, with their book-length format containing sequential art narrative, make a different set of requirements on both the physiology and intellect of the reader. In order to read a graphic novel, one must be literate in both text and visual cues, able to interpret what a picture "says" and relate that content to text, while being sensitive to how image and word stand in relationship to each other on the page.

WHAT IS A GRAPHIC NOVEL?

The graphic novel, as a narrative publication, can be found on the continuum of sequential art that also comprises comic strips, comic books, and Latin American *fotonovelas*. In that continuum, the comic strip presents a single idea—often but not always a joke or gag—that unfolds across several panels (usually three to five). Comic books contain multipage— and typically multi-issue—stories that are published as serials; more often than not, comic books are the work of multiple artists and writers working for a studio or working with characters created by some agency beyond themselves. The *fotonovela* may be comic book–like in its serial nature, or closed-ended, as is the graphic novel, but it is told through camera snapshots rather than drawing.

The graphic novel shares many physical and aesthetic characteristics with other formats in this continuum, of course. It differs by being a bounded narrative, with a story arc that has a beginning, middle, and end (although often across more than a single bound volume, especially outside Anglo-American publishing). It is a format capable of containing a wide range of genres—including nonfiction—for a wide range of ages. Awkwardly, the term currently encompasses works of fact as well as fiction and, in many public and school libraries, has been further expanded to be inclusive of bound volumes of reprinted comic book series.

The history of sequential art in the forms of comics and cartooning is relatively long when compared to that of the graphic novel. While the term *graphic novel* was first applied by Will Eisner just thirty years ago, to his *A Contract with God*, books with graphic novel–like attributes were published elsewhere in the world earlier in the twentieth century.[1] Belgian Hergé's children's stories about Tintin, first published before World War II, boast a series cast but each book contains a complete story arc; in this regard, Tintin might be compared with the same era's American Hardy Boys or Nancy Drew, in which each book recounts an adventure that is independent of other titles in which the various juvenile detectives star.[2] In Japan, Osamu Tezuka wrote manga, or Japanese comic books, but also an eight-volume sequential art biography of Siddhartha Gautama (the Buddha), on which he worked for a decade, beginning in 1974.[3]

Like many other sequential art narratives, the graphic novel presents itself through the combined forces of image and word. Images here are not illustrations that simply repeat or amplify text, but rather carry information not revealed verbally. Correspondingly, the verbal content provides information not present in the image; it is not a caption. Most typically, image and text are brought together within panels or defined spaces on the page, but in some instances the entire page may serve as a panel.[4]

In some cases, the graphic novel may be wordless. However, even where this is the case—such as in some of the works of Belgian Frans Masereel (1899–1972)—the images are arranged in the same linear fashion as would be verbal text, providing a beginning, middle, and end to a story arc.[5]

READING A GRAPHIC NOVEL

In order to read a graphic novel, one must exercise multiple literacies. The text requires traditional decoding skills, while the images require the reader to interpret facial and body language as well as the use of white space and shading, and be oriented to the flow of panels as they carry the narrative forward. In addition, one must work within both literacies at the same time, approaching the text with facility to apprehend word and image synchronically.

The graphic novel reader creates the actual moment of any action in his or her imagination, because the panel images are static. The graphic novel shares many conventions found in film—and the writing of graphic novels and other sequential art forms includes "scripting" the narrative—but it is, after all, static ink on a page. Because our eyes and imaginations are closely bound to experience, when we perceive that placement in one panel differs from that in the next, we are barely conscious of filling in the action that must have occurred.

Because a graphic novel is a bounded, linear narrative, the reader begins at one end of it and progresses—typically left to right, top to bottom—page by page. Although the publication of manga in English now is likely to occur with the flow remaining intact as moving from right to left (as it does in Japanese), the essential tenet remains true: unlike a volume of collected cartoon strips the reader might browse by opening at any point and skipping down and up the page, traditional tracking skills, as applied to text-only books, are the rule with graphic novels.[6] (There are pages in some graphic novels that are arranged to bring the reader's eye immediately to the center, but there are pages of text-only poetry that promote the same physiological pull. In both instances, this refocusing of the typical reading path carries a message related to the text at hand.)

APPEAL FACTORS ASSOCIATED WITH GRAPHIC NOVELS

Readers' advisory theory has expanded in recent years to codify a variety of appeal factors, the aesthetic scent that allures individual readers (or repels or wafts by unnoticed for others). The Readers' Advisory Committees of the Reference and User Services Association's Collection Development and Evaluation Section (RUSA/CODES) and the Public Library Association set up a joint committee to develop appeal categories that reflect attributes of narrative nonfiction; classifications of such attributes include pace, setting, character, skill enhancement, tone, topic, and so forth. Public librarians in the United Kingdom have created a database of readers' advice that draws on gradations of such appeal factors as humor, satisfaction, predictability, length, and degree of difficulty.[7] Both of these efforts to identify specific elements that prove attractive to some readers do much to inform the possibilities for providing reader advice relevant to graphic novels.

But there are appeal factors specific to the graphic novel format as well. The most obvious is format itself: graphic novels are necessarily visual as well as necessarily verbal. Not all graphic novel readers are *primarily* visual by nature, however. One can be "wired"—as each of us seems to be with a preference for one or another specific means of input—to prefer auditory perception, but be an ardent graphic novel reader. However, it is likely that someone who is primarily auditory in orientation will be drawn to graphic novels with which auditory preference is harmonious: more linearity, fewer intricate images, etc. Most basically, the appeal factors that graphic novels share with traditional format narratives include

- plot
- language (visual as well as verbal)
- character
- style
- length
- subject
- difficulty
- predictability
- outlook
- conventionality

And in addition to the added appeal of visual or auditory preference, there is another appeal category unique to graphic novels in the book world, but not in the larger universe of storytelling. Because the graphic novel *is* visual and because image conveys to our gut in a way that mere text does not, we must add the appeal category of *visceral pull* to the list.

The visceral pull also occurs when we watch films and listen to audiobooks or professional storytellers. On occasion, it happens when we attend staged plays, though the convention of the stage and ranked seating of an audience regularly intervenes between our eyes and our gut. The play may be very good, but it is not the same as seeing an unexpected drama in the street (although some staging—such as when actors walk into the audience—can collapse the distance). When we watch a filmed scene— whether it is beautiful or hideous, the unfolding of a magnificent event or the record of a violent encounter—the occlusion of aesthetic space plays to our gut; we feel what we see and we feel it personally. Similarly, listening to well-produced aural literature collapses distance between the verbal content and our inner sense of space.

So, too, with sequential art. While the comic strip is too brief to pull us—gut and all—into its space, comic books and graphic novels are long enough to collapse personal space by virtue of what we see. This may appeal to us in some circumstances, with some types of narratives, and thus the visceral pull must be counted as a factor for the graphic novel reader to experience or eschew or choose in varying instances.

Like all appeal factors, those related to graphic novel reading and appreciation are scalable. In sum, these scales follow the same continua along which traditional format narratives can be tracked:

- plot: including type, complexity, and importance to narrative
- language: both verbal and visual, in degree of complexity and richness
- character: type and, like plot, relative importance to narrative
- style: both verbal and visual
- length: from brief to great
- subject: including genre but also more specific topics
- difficulty: degree of effort needed to "enter" the narrative
- predictability: from expected to unexpected in its unfolding
- outlook: from positive or optimistic to negative or pessimistic
- conventionality: playing to or against narrative tradition, by any degree
- visceral effect: type as well as degree

WHO NEEDS TO DO GRAPHIC NOVEL READERS' ADVISORY WORK?

Readers' advisory work is being undertaken in libraries of all types, with varying degrees of active and passive methods. At the same time, the graphic novel has become an accepted format in an increasing number of library types. Therefore, it seems clear that anywhere readers are served with professional reading advice, those performing the service need to include the format in their repertoires.

In situations where reading advice is passive, taking the form of lists, shelf-talk cards, and other make-ahead tools, the library may be able to depend on a relatively small staff to create graphic novel readers' advisory enhancements. Where active advice is provided, however—and this is likely to be something the community seeks once passive means of advising are in place—staff charged with providing reader services should be able to speak to graphic novels just as they can to other formats.

EDUCATING NEW GRAPHIC NOVEL READERS' ADVISORS

As with any type of book, being a graphic novel reader is not the single condition that can make an adequate, to say nothing of an excellent, advisor to others seeking assistance in making reading selections. However, being able to read and feel some literate enthusiasm for the format is a necessary first step to becoming an advisor.

The first technical detail the advisor needs to learn is that graphic novels are a format rather than a genre, a container rather than a type of plot. Depending on the individual advisor's own taste in reading, learning to read and appreciate the textures and variety of graphic novels is best begun by choosing first those books that match the advisor's usual personal reading choices. Biography? Mystery? Best seller? Literary fiction? Each of these qualifications can be explored within the graphic novel format, assuring the new readers' advisor that the format can fit personal interest.

We live in a culture and a time where browsing has become increasingly popular and quick, especially where images are concerned. Reports announce the decline of reading newspaper articles in full in favor of grazing headlines and initial paragraphs online. With a visual book format, this can mean the new graphic novel readers' advisor, in training mode, may assume that a casual browse through a few pages of representative books will sufficiently acquaint him with the feel and effect of the format. However, if the advisor is truly seeking clarification of how the format works for the reader, such an approach cheats him—as well as future clients. Just as one cannot understand how imagery, symbolism, and style unfold in the short stories of Ernest Hemingway or Flannery O'Connor without actually reading several in full, one needs to allow graphic novels to reveal themselves by reading them fully.

Because reading the format requires one to attend to both image and verbal content, picture grazing simply won't do. An advisor who is familiar with specific creators' styles may be able to provide casual recommendations without reading specific titles closely, but the new graphic novel advisor can expand his repertoire in this format best through full consideration of a large sample of books.

WHAT'S NEXT ...

In the following chapter, we'll discuss various ways to present advice about which graphic novel might be a good next book to read, both to individuals seeking active advice and to the general community to which we present more passive reading advice.

Notes

1. Will Eisner, *A Contract with God* (New York: Baronet Press, 1978).
2. Hergé, The Adventures of Tintin series, beginning with *Tintin in the Land of the Soviets* (San Francisco: Last Gasp, 2003).
3. Osamu Tezuka, *Buddha* (New York: Vertical, 2003–2005).
4. For a thorough and informative discussion of comics and graphic novel anatomy, see Scott McCloud's classic *Understanding Comics: The Invisible Art* (New York: HarperPerennial, 1994) and his *Making Comics: Storytelling Secrets of Comics, Manga and Graphic Novels* (New York: Harper, 2006).
5. For examples of the wordless novels by Masereel and others, see the reprinting of several in *Graphic Witness: Four Wordless Graphic Novels* (Cambridge, MA: Firefly Books, 2007).
6. Within this decade, the American publication of manga in translation has increasingly come with the maintenance of the original's right-to-left orientation. This has been undertaken to allow the integrity of the artwork to remain true to Japanese conventions, rather than being "flipped" to suit left-to-right English language writing conventions.
7. Whichbook, www.whichbook.net/default.aspx.

2
PUSHING GRAPHIC NOVEL ADVICE TO READERS

I n this chapter, we'll explore both active and passive methods of providing advice to graphic novel readers and potential graphic novel
readers. As with reading advice of any sort, some people seek personal interaction while others prefer to find clues and directions in the
landscape.

GRAPHIC NOVEL READING ADVICE AS PART
OF A BIGGER ADVISING PICTURE

The art and practice of readers' advisory work has enjoyed a renaissance
over the past fifteen years. Mary Kay Chelton has focused the attention of
both youth services providers and public library staffs more generally on
the shortfalls too many readers have found when asking for reading advice
at the library.[1] Joyce Saricks has provided useful advice to make us better
respondents and theory to expand our understanding of the whys behind
reading advice–seeking behavior.[2] During the Public Library Association's
11th Biannual Conference in 2006, Neal Wyatt, Georgine Olson, and their
colleagues turned our attention to the fact that the desire for reading advice
isn't limited to fiction or a hunger for book lists.[3] Staff at the Williams-
burg (Virginia) Regional Library are blazing trails in reconceiving advising
strategies so that immediate—but perhaps less than thorough—gratifica-
tion is replaced with a model of intake, analysis, and suggestions intended
to keep the reader occupied through multiple library visits.[4]

Readers of many genre and nonfiction interests continue to assume
that folks who work in libraries know books and thus can help in a search

for something good to read. At the same time, relatively few library staff members are recognized by this same general public as being knowledge-able enough about graphic novels to be helpful as advisors. This is chang-ing, and may not be true in your community—or, at least, not among read-ers who have come to know you as an advisor—but dedicated graphic novel readers on the whole still turn to the Web, to their local comics shops, and to friends who share their reading interests rather than the library staff as potential advisors.

In the earlier burgeoning of librarian concern with readers' advisory work, which blossomed in the second and third decades of the twentieth century, those seeking advice tended to be less well-schooled than those from whom they sought the advice. The public library acted—as it contin-ues to act—as the poor person's (and immigrant's) university; the librar-ian was recognized as a lead authority within that venue.[5] Although this remains true for some library users in some communities, perhaps some of the time those seeking reading advice from the contemporary librar-ian are more likely to see themselves as being on equal, or nearly equal, footing in terms of intellectual ability. The librarian may be perceived as knowing the names and rhetorical characteristics of a markedly greater number of mystery writers, romance series, or even sea-going biographies than does the reader in the street, but that reader in the street continues to assume that that broader and deeper knowledge is a kind of personal foible—the same foible that led the librarian to decide to take up a library career and thus be around books—than as a skill professionally honed and continuously refined for the benefit of the public. (Of course, this is not true in all communities. Lucky the librarian who works with a public that recognizes that professionals who work with books and information have training, skill, and dedication analogous to professionals who work with building plans or dental health.)

With the exception of young children who are still innocent enough to assume that adults are experts in most things, individuals who read and would appreciate advice on what graphic novels to read next are not likely to assume that librarians know graphic novels the way they know police procedurals, travel literature, or inspirational titles. Turning around this general impression may take several more years, but it is a case of thinking globally and acting locally. If you want and plan to be a graphic novel readers' advisor, start advising rather than waiting for the recogni-tion that you have that kind of reading advice to give.

PERSONAL ENCOUNTERS WITH READERS

One archetypal method of delivering readers' advisory services within a library is through personal encounter. A patron approaches a staff member—sometimes a clearly designated "Readers' Advisor" ensconced in a vast reading room but more often a circulation assistant or shelver—and requests assistance in identifying something appealing. The RUSA/CODES Readers' Advisory Committee's contributions to the theory of appeal factors should be required reading for anyone staffing a library.[6] Library users aren't likely to refer to them obliquely, but library staff who are familiar with these appeal factors have a markedly easier time conducting the necessary traditional interview in order to separate the advisor's enthusiasms from the inquirer's.[7]

Library staff who regularly provide this type of personal readers' advisory work recognize patrons' opinions as valuable when advising other patrons. Nancy Pearl notwithstanding, few staff members (but every library seems to have one) can manage to read as widely and without prejudice as would suit the desires of readers hoping to glean truly personal advice and reading suggestions based on our own reading pleasures. What we can't ingest firsthand or borrow from reviews and browsing, other patrons often can supply when they talk books with us.

Providing readers' advisory assistance in this direct way to someone on the prowl for graphic novels does require the advisor to have some (positive) experience with the format. Imagine a would-be advisor attempting to assist a patron in selecting some DVDs for the weekend if the advisor had never watched a movie, or had seen one once and hadn't much cared for its content. You have to have experienced the format in order to know what could possibly matter to or engage your advice seeker. "Experience" doesn't mean you've read a dozen examples but, as with movies, you've investigated and experienced widely enough firsthand to have a feel for styles, a sense of what you yourself like and don't like in the medium and why, and how to read, or listen to, reviews of titles you will never read in toto in a way that allows you to have a sense of what appeals they might have.

How do you find readers of graphic novels whom you don't see browsing the graphic novel collection (if your library provides specific shelving for it) or checking out graphic novels? Include attention to graphic novels in the interviewing you conduct with all of those seeking reading advice. Don't limit this reference to the format to patrons of a particular age group (unless your library collects graphic novels and comics for only one age group) or to readers who bring it up first. If you've got someone in front of you wanting biographies about British commoners, include Briggs's *Ethel and Ernest* in your suggestions.[8] If the patron is interested in becoming acquainted with literary classics and wants to be steered toward some she'll find immediately interesting and readable, think to include volumes from editor Tom Pomplun's Graphic Classics series.[9]

If you do get to discuss graphic novels regularly with clients who are already dedicated readers in the format, be sure to find out their opinions about titles you know you're unlikely to read thoroughly yourself. And pay attention to what other books these graphic novel enthusiasts are reading, so that when you suggest that particular science fiction author or poet to someone for whom graphic novels aren't on the horizon, you can suggest a graphic novel or two that your graphic novel–friendly patron was also reading.

BOOK DISPLAYS

Book displays are among the most popular and endemic forms of passive reading advice provided in libraries. Whether the display is as formal and flashy as a stage set with added scenery—posters, realia—or pedestrian but popular as the new bookshelf right by the door, material placed here will catch the attention it is likely to miss when shelved in its cataloging- and architecture-driven place in the stacks. Including displays of graphic novels in the library's rotation of highlighted materials is fine. Better is to include some graphic novels in any topical or thematic book display. Collecting books to display on survivors' stories? Be sure to include Brabner, Pekar, and Stack's *Our Cancer Year* and Mack's *Janet and Me.*[10] Celebrating Presidents' Day? Geary's *The Murder of Abraham Lincoln* belongs in that set of books.[11] Literary awards? Don't forget to include representative winners of the Eisner, the Harvey, and France's Prix Alpha-Art.[12]

Too often, book displays leave viewers to judge books by their covers, or even just by their spines. When including graphic novels in your displays, include a photocopied page or two from each title to show off the art and the page flow. If the book is printed in color, spend a little extra and make a color copy of the page so that passersby get a true sense of what the book has to offer that might suit—or even pique—their interest. Of course, you'll need to select the pages you are displaying wisely. Not only do you want to avoid showing any violence or adult situations to passersby, you want to keep such scenes from being viewed out of context. Beyond that cautionary reason for making a well-chosen selection to display, you also want to present passersby with a fair understanding of how this or that particular graphic novel flows: choose a page layout on which the panels are arranged typically for that title, where no plot surprise is given away, and, if possible, where any main character might be depicted.

MEDIA TIE-INS

In recent years, not only tried-and-true comic book series but some independent and stand-alone graphic novels are enjoying filmmakers' attentions. Be sure to draw readers' attention to the graphic novels in your collections that are the basis for, or run parallel to, such media sensations. Does your library have a film license that allows you to show movies on a regular basis? Include a program or two that feature films based on the works of Harvey Pekar, Daniel Clowes, and Jerry Siegel and Joe Shuster.[13]

Beyond film, track and exploit other media tie-ins. Does your community sponsor or have devotees affiliated with various AIDS benefit activities such as long-distance bicycle rides? If you've got a staff member participating, angle a mention of Winick's *Pedro and Me* into the human interest story you'll want your local paper or cable station to run about her involvement.[14]

Be sure to hype your newest graphic novel acquisitions whenever the community newspaper wants to feature a soft news story about services or programs at your library. You don't have to use a sledgehammer to bring home the fact that you've got graphic novels and want to help readers find the ones they'll like. Just include a reference to a specific title that suits the rest of the article. A feature story on the children's summer reading game? Include the Asterix series by Goscinny and Uderzo or Tanaka's *Wings* in your list of books waiting for kids to discover them.[15] A notice appearing that your library now circulates Japanese language books? An obvious note to include is that in addition to classics, cookbooks, and manuals on sewing projects, the collection offers three new shelves of manga.

BOOKTALKS

If you regularly provide booktalks to schools, to civic organizations, or during in-house programs, include graphic novels appropriate to the theme and interests of the audience. Be sure to expand any graphic novel–heavy booktalk series with additional books detailing techniques or biographical information about the selected artists. Booktalks are an excellent way to alert potential readers to the fact that books are more varied than what they might imagine. Not only young people, but older adults, too, may be startled to discover that not every set of covers opens onto small black print in even rows across endless pages.

Certainly graphic novels dispose themselves nicely to visual presentations. When booktalking live in front of a group, select graphic novels that are large enough for everyone to be able to appreciate the images and panel flow of an open page spread. Choose the page spread you will share beforehand so that you don't provide the rude surprise of flashing a group unexpected nudity or scenes of violence. Context is important; what works and is appropriate when one is reading a book in its entirety can be shocking and off-putting if displayed without the context the author or artist has provided.

If you do want to share a graphic novel that is small, prepare for the booktalk by finding a relatively unembellished image or panel and photocopying an enlargement of it. This will allow the group to get a view of the artist's style. Allow your audience to leaf through the books after your talk. This is always a good tactic when you want to get books into the audience's hands, but with graphic novels, the need to feel the flow of any particular book is urgent.

Using podcasting, PowerPoint, or other presentation software, some libraries have taken booktalks onto their websites. Instead of lists of suggested books of one theme or another, these presentations allow the viewer a more intimate preview of the suggested books.

If you are booktalking graphic novels to a group in which there is already a confirmed graphic novel reader or two, garner their support through recommendations of additional titles the rest of the audience may find appealing. Don't undermine your own show by giving the cognoscenti the opportunity to debate your choices, but rather invite them to build from these to additional titles.

BOOK CLUBS/BOOK DISCUSSION GROUPS

Whether your library book group is most interested in classics, books in Spanish, current events, or popular culture, there are graphic novels you can suggest for their upcoming reading calendars. If you or someone in your community would like to sponsor a graphic novels–only book group, be sure that the ages of group members are such that all can enjoy read-ing and discussing the same graphic novels. While a seventh-grader may comfortably participate in a typically adult book group discussion of San-dra Cisneros's *The House on Mango Street,* she would be an unlikely candi-date to be present in an adult discussion of the Love and Rockets series by Los Bros Hernandez.[16]

In book discussions where the subject is a graphic novel, be sure to elicit and incorporate participants' views on the flavor and use of images, panel flows, and other attributes that set off the book as a graphic novel and different from a traditional text title. Ask questions about artistic style, the use of viewpoint in the images as a narrative device, and any symbol-ism (for example, color) that the images provide.

AWARDS LISTS

Many libraries post lists of literary awards in prominent locations. Like best seller lists, these lists are recognized by most library visitors as use-ful suggestions because the titles on them have the blessing of authority (or high sales!). If you've got a graphic novel collection in your library, then post lists of both winners and shortlisted titles and authors. Relevant annual lists include the Eisner Awards, the Harvey Awards, and some-times even the Pulitzers and the Nebula Awards. See chapter 8 for a list of awards to follow and promote.

Don't post such lists just near the graphic novels. If you want to open your readers to the possibility of adding this format to their reading rep-ertoire, highlight the lists in the same places you post traditional literary award lists: at the information desk, near the returns area, or at the new book displays. Additionally, make sure you announce the short lists and ultimate winners on your library's web page. If possible, link those online lists to your own OPAC so browsers are led directly to the fact that you've got the goods that are making the buzz.

WHAT'S NEXT . . .

In the following chapter, we'll discuss ways an advisor can connect with readers who already feel an affinity for the graphic novel format. These readers may be easier for some traditional libraries to serve, because they have stated needs to which the advisor may react, rather than pre-senting situations in which the advisor must be proactive in bringing

attention to the format. We'll discuss the aesthetics of graphic novel literature and then advisory work with children, teens, and adults as three specific demographic groups of graphic novel readers who can benefit from
good advice.

Notes

1. Mary Kay Chelton, "What We Know and Don't Know about Reading, Readers, and Readers' Advisory Services," *Public Libraries* (February 1999): 42–47.
2. Joyce Saricks and Nancy Brown, *Readers' Advisory Service in the Public Library*, 2nd ed. (Chicago: American Library Association, 2001).
3. See handouts for sessions 187 and others held during PLA 2006, www.placonference .org/2006/handouts_audiotapes.cfm.
4. "Looking for a Good Book?" at www.wrl.org/bookweb/RA/index.html. This is a web-based form that interested readers complete in the degree of detail that best suits each one. Staff analyzes an individual's appeals and tastes and compiles a custom suggested reading list.
5. *ALA World Encyclopedia of Library and Information Services* (Chicago: American Library Association, 1986).
6. "Narrative Nonfiction: What's the Appeal?" presented April 24, 2007, at the New Jersey Library Association (www.njla.org/conference/2007/presentations/ NarrativeNonfiction.pdf). Barry Trott discusses the appeal factors developed by RUSA/CODES and presented at the PLA conference held two years earlier.
7. In *Readers' Advisor News,* June 2005 (http://lu.com/ranews/june2005/orr.cfm), Cindy Orr includes this as number 7 in her Golden Rules of Readers' Advisory Service: "Readers want a book that is right for *them*. Resist the temptation to talk about your favorite book or the book you are reading now. Put yourself into the readers' shoes and try to understand what *they* might like . . . what would appeal to *them*, and not what you yourself enjoy—or even worse, what you think they *should* read."
8. Raymond Briggs, *Ethel and Ernest: A True Story* (New York: Knopf, 1999).
9. Eureka Productions of Mt. Horeb, Wisconsin, publishes a lengthening series of anthologies featuring the works of Bram Stoker, Edgar Allan Poe, Ambrose Bierce, H. G. Wells, and others. Each volume includes contributions by various cartoonists along with selections from the original author's writings.
10. Joyce Brabner, Harvey Pekar, and Frank Stack, *Our Cancer Year* (New York: Four Walls Eight Windows, 1994); Stan Mack, *Janet and Me: An Illustrated Story of Love and Loss* (New York: Simon and Schuster, 2004).
11. Rick Geary, *The Murder of Abraham Lincoln: A Chronicle of 62 Days in the Life of the American Republic, March 4–May 4, 1865* (New York: NBM, ComicsLit, 2005).
12. To check on both past and current winners of the diverse awards presented to graphic novels and comics artists, see the *Comic Book Awards Almanac* (http://users.rcn.com/ aardy/comics/awards/).
13. Pekar's work is the inspiration for *American Splendor;* Clowes wrote not only the graphic novel but the movie script for *Ghost World;* Siegel and Shuster are the Cleveland high school boys who invented Superman nearly seventy-five years ago.
14. Judd Winick, *Pedro and Me: Friendship, Loss, and What I Learned* (New York: Henry Holt, 2000).
15. Asterix by Goscinny and Uderzo, the long-running series of cartoon history adventures undertaken by a first-century Gaul and his sidekicks, is now being republished by Orion (2004–), and distributed in the United States by the Sterling Publishing

Company. *Wings* by Shinsuke Tanaka (Port Washington, NY: Purple Bear Books, 2006) is a nearly wordless story with broad appeal across age groups.

16. Sandra Cisneros, *The House on Mango Street* (New York: Knopf, 1991). Los Bros Hernandez—Gilbert and Jaime Hernandez—wrote a long-running series of stories in the Love and Rockets comics, published by Fantagraphics (Seattle) beginning in 1982. On their own, the brothers have been publishing prodigious graphic novels and graphic novel story collections, also with Fantagraphics.

3
MOVING COMICS READERS FROM ONE GRAPHIC NOVEL TO THE NEXT

Readers who already know they enjoy graphic novels may not directly seek advice on what to read next. Although libraries have been building graphic novel and comics collections with gusto in recent years, fewer library staff members present themselves—and, in turn, are recognized—as conversant and comfortable with the format than the number who are likely to provide advice in genre fiction.

AGE PERCEPTION IS STILL A PROBLEM

The American equation of sequential art reading with juvenilia persists in the assumptions and underlying processes of many public and school libraries. While publishers and bookstores recognize and address the graphic novel reading interests of adults, and, increasingly, very young children, libraries regularly ghettoize their graphic novel collections in youth departments.

This speaks volumes to adult readers. Why seek advice from an institution where your reading tastes either go unrecognized or seem to be marginalized?

Before planning a sophisticated approach to augmenting the experiences of graphic novel readers, then, the library needs to assess its collection placements, both on shelf and online. Are readers of adult graphic novels welcome? Are their age-specific skills and experiences recognized? Are the materials housed in young adult collections age appropriate, or has the young adult collection become the only safe haven for any graphic novels in the library's collection, without due regard to their fit with the age and interests of the community's teens?

RESPECT FOR READING DIVERSITY

How are confirmed graphic novel readers perceived by library staff? Are children who read comics presumed to be doing so as a way station in their literacy development, rather than as a specific arrival point? Are teens and adults who seek graphic novels assumed to be reluctant readers, intellectually stunted, or lazy? Such judgments are both harsh and ill-placed. As librarians, our role in connecting the reader with books is not to assume capacity as an output of taste. Such judgments tell more about the library staff member's lack of familiarity with formats, genres, and literary options than serve as an accurate measure of community members' desire to find books worth reading.

YES, VIRGINIA, AESTHETICS DO MATTER

The philosophy of aesthetics as presented by several notable theoreticians can be used to inform a systematic view of graphic novel reader appreciation.[1] In her mid-twentieth-century work, Susanne K. Langer offers researchers a taut analysis of symbolism and its relationship to each of the arts, mining both the visual and narrative elements that compose the graphic novel, although without recognizing comics in and of themselves.[2] Roland Barthes, a French aesthetics and semiology scholar who notably spent much of his mature academic life working in Japan, has written extensively and compellingly on the uses of image in thought and communication, culture and identity.[3] Thomas Berger, a novelist as well as a theoretician concerned directly with consciousness and image, treats vision and imagination as two access points between the individual and his world, one relying on the other in an eternal conversation.[4]

The point here is not that reading graphic novels is a difficult or academic matter, but rather that advising graphic novel readers cannot be sloughed off as unnecessary service in a library where other forms of literature are honored and where advising is taken seriously. Working with readers who already appreciate the format can help the new graphic novel readers' advisor to reach a clearer and more accurate understanding of the format as part of the literary and artistic continuum. Experienced graphic novel reader/advisors, on the other hand, can mine interviews with other enthusiasts to reach increasingly critical understandings of taste and craft.

HELPING THE GRAPHIC NOVEL READER RECOGNIZE
THE WHY IN WHAT SHE CHOOSES

In the first chapter, we discussed the variety of appeal categories that come into play when considering one or another graphic novel in relation to one or another reader. When offering reading advice to someone who knows the format, the advisor may well need to help delineate the specific aspects of the format—and choices within the format—that appeal to this particular reader. Talking about favorite titles in terms of appeal categories is a straightforward way of approaching advisory work, but it is not always—or even often—the easiest route for readers who know what they like but aren't accustomed to analyzing which details make up the whole that they appreciate.

Theme lists provide access to some of these appeal categories, but typically describe either the genre or subject matter of titles on the lists, rather than supplying vocabulary that names such compelling appeal details as

- visual style
- layout
- image/text balance
- supporting work

Let's take a look at each of these concerns.

Visual Style

Any graphic novel enthusiast probably has a predilection for some styles and difficulty with others. One reader may eschew stories that are told with monochromatic tones or gray-scale washes as simply visually unappealing, while another may enjoy such works for their visual subtlety. A quantity of visual detail may intrude for some readers, while being an enjoyable feature for others.

There are a variety of canonical visual styles associated with graphic novels. While many graphic novel readers select broadly among these visual styles, talking about the styles with the inquiring reader can help the advisor better understand what appeals to this person at this time. Visual styles include (but certainly aren't limited to!)

> Clear line (Hergé's Tintin, Clément Oubrerie's artwork in *Aya* by Marguerite Abouet) offers full-color images with bounded areas for each hue. Often, works depicted in this visual style include such naturalistic elements as people and animals, plants and weather.[5]

> Soft pencil, charcoal, and ink washes (Joe Kubert's *Yossel, April 19, 1943: A Story of the Warsaw Ghetto Uprising*, Posy Simmonds's

Tamara Drewe) make for soft, subtle shadings in which details may be blurred or liable to exposure accompanied by surprise.[6]

Black ink (Marjane Satrapi's *Persepolis,* Ande Parks and Chris Samnee's *Capote in Kansas*) provides two opposite tones: black and (usually) white, which together give images a flatness and can offer a heightened visual tension.[7]

Block print, scratch board, or other emulations of past printing styles (Charles Burns's *Black Hole,* Peter Kuper's treatments of Franz Kafka's fiction, including *Give It Up: And Other Short Stories*), while also typically black and white, introduce both a retro viewpoint and a dramatization of angles.[8]

Water coloring/colored ink (Lewis Trondheim's *Little Nothings,* and other of his books) is close to clear line but less flat, as the coloring lacks the bounded fields for each hue, and thus can suggest more dimensionality.[9]

Computer enhanced, or digital images (Ho Che Anderson's *King,* Paul Pope's *Heavy Liquid*) exploit the possibilities for binding media in singular images.[10]

And within manga, which is almost always largely black and white, there are a variety of standard visual styles, including

realistic (with emotions and fantasies depicted with less realistic proportions and the inclusion of symbolism)

soft and rounded (as you might expect in cartoons for young readers)

highly stylized, even sketchy (denoting a harder edge to the story)

The coda of manga is extensive and is treated best, in descriptive terms, by specialists such as Jason Thomson in his *Manga: The Complete Guide* or Robin Brenner in her *Understanding Manga and Anime.*[11] See appendix B for the rudiments of types and styles of manga, as well as translation issues, including panel order and standard symbolism, that the beginning graphic novel readers' advisor with no prior experience of manga must grasp.

Beyond the elements of color and drawing style, visual components include type size and style, the relation between design space and white space, and the degree of visual detail. While the various combinations of these elements aren't likely to rise to the awareness of the reader, the astute readers' advisor needs to take all visual aspects into consideration when analyzing a particular work's appeal.

Type size appeal may be the most purely physical of appeal categories: readers who are uncomfortable with focusing on a font that is too small or too far from plain simply can't enjoy reading it. White space, too, can aid a reader who has difficulty with physical focus, providing a "relief field" for eyes that otherwise become strained.

The amount and quality of detail rendered within the images of a particular graphic novel is an appeal component that can be mined with great satisfaction. Does the reader enjoy simple images to which his or her imagination adds the furniture of minute detail, as in Adam Sacks's *Salmon Doubts*?[12] Or does the reader prefer visuals that incorporate vast amounts of depiction of detail, such as period wallpaper prints (Rick Geary's *The Borden Tragedy*), or character information (Brian Wood and Ryan Kelly's *Local*)?[13]

Layout

In addition to overall drawing styles, visual elements of a graphic novel include layout, which necessarily includes a visual aspect. However, layout moves beyond the purely visual to speak to intellectual appeal as it calls upon the reader to track narrative flow in a particular way, and can be more or less demanding than other schematic arrangements of content.

While older comic books, with their immediate ancestry in comic strips, tended to offer the reader pages on which panels were laid out left to right, top to bottom, layout can now require the reader to gather images by fusing panels (Sabrina Jones's *Isadora Duncan*) or bring the reader's eye to the center of the page for a passage's dramatic culmination (Craig Thompson's *Good-bye, Chunky Rice*).[14] When reading an essentially visual narrative, preferences may develop in page tracking, just as there may be preferences for great or lesser visual detail. It's important to note that such preferences are aesthetic and should not be judged as *sophisticated* or *underdeveloped* any more than the advisor would think to judge a devotee of blank verse poetry as more or less sophisticated than someone who prefers sonnets.

Image/Text Balance

We know from considerable psychological and educational work undertaken across the past forty years that, like left- and right-handed dominance, some individuals are predisposed to access the world with visual dominance, auditory dominance, or kinesthetic dominance. This predisposition may well influence their reading preferences.

For instance, readers who tend to learn about their surroundings and attend to their world primarily through auditory stimuli relate to written narrative by "hearing" the text as they read. Visual people, on the other hand, are stimulated more intensely by the patterns of print. In neither case is the reader aware of the dominance as she reads. This is not a conscious effort any more than the right-handed person's reach for a pen with which to endorse a check is self-conscious and considered.

Readers with any of these dominant predispositions may enjoy graphic novels, but the *how* of their enjoyment may differ. The auditorially dominant reader may be led through the narrative text-first, while the visually dominant may find himself moving image-first. This does not mean that the reader prone to auditory dominance reads only the text and eschews the images; to do so wouldn't be to read the graphic novel, which requires the lexical uncovering of text and image together to create a whole.

What it does mean is that some readers are likely to prefer one level of balance between text and image while others may prefer an alternative balance. This is parallel to one reader preferring convoluted sentence structure to another preferring the pithy—such as Faulkner versus Hemingway. Neither is *simpler* but each presents a different appeal quality.

Supporting Work

Some graphic novel readers are drawn to the medium as an enhancement of other media, such as movies or games. (We will address that avenue of interest flowing between the format and related formats in chapter 5.) However, readers may also be drawn to graphic novels that provide sequential art treatment of content that has no specific animated correlative.

Sometimes the supporting work is synonymous with the graphic novel's subject or theme. One reader may have a particular taste for graphic novels that expose realistic scenes in a realistic plot, while another has a conscious preference for accessing biography in a sequential art medium in which details of the subject (for instance, left-handedness) are revealed and snippets of the subject's own words are captured within the text. However, the appreciation of supporting work may also arise from the reader's affinity for French or Japanese popular culture, knowing that comics play a role in these experiences, or an author who writes in both the sequential art and print narrative worlds (such as Neil Gaiman).

BEYOND APPEAL TO INTEREST

Appeal alone does not create inveterate graphic novel readers. Exposure over a period of time to an array of possibilities that includes titles without as well as with personal appeal helps to shape a reader's interest in (and dedication to) specific subjects, formats, and genres. Advising the dedicated graphic novel reader requires a deep and broad awareness of what is and has been available as reading choices. The dedicated graphic novel reader may inhabit a genre niche—experienced with and aware of only specific genres within the format—or may be an omnivorous consumer of the format, aware of a variety of genres. It's necessary as an advisor to find out these details, rather than assuming that the reader already devoted to comics might be devoted to any or all sequential art stories.

Interest is correlated to access. Moving a reader who has demonstrable appreciation for one or another area of the sequential art publishing universe to other parts of it requires the advisor to be able to communicate similarities and differences. The teenager who is a dedicated shojo manga reader is one who finds emotions and, perhaps, character, more appealing than action and, perhaps, plot construction. Providing her with reading advice that expands upon the awareness and taste she already recognizes in herself requires the advisor to analyze possibilities in terms of the emotional content they offer. Another reader, with a stated taste for gritty realism, would profit from advice that recognizes that realism can be fictional as well as journalistic, and that both are available within the format.

The interested reader is also the reader more likely to be susceptible to learning about his own tastes, the one who may find enjoyment in discussing appeal elements in a manner that allows for growth in his own metacognition of why one book attracts while another seems to bode a slog. To be able to provide this reader with sound advice, the advisor also needs to be experienced with interest, not only aware of appeal elements.

DISCUSSING INTEREST

Talking about graphic novels with those already interested in reading more, or different, possibilities, demands that the advisor be prepared to consider possible appeal elements, availability of both exemplary and additional titles, and the reader's own statements about preferences, concerns, and reading history. Among the questions the advisor hopes to plumb, although not always with a direct interview, are

- What appeals to you most about your favorite graphic novel?
- What content or subject most interests you?
- How familiar are you with current titles? With older ones?
- What manner of complexity appeals to you?
- Where do you place yourself, as the reader, relative to the sequential art text as it unfolds?

The first of these questions has been treated in the previous chapter, while the second and third ones are not format-specific and would be important in a readers' advisory interview of any sort. We will then move on to discuss the relevancy of the fourth and fifth questions.

Complexity as a Matter of Appeal

Many types of art, including various types of books, draw on an audience's interest in degrees of complexity. Complexity in a straight-text work generally refers to plotting, syntax, and/or vocabulary. In sequential art, complexity may reference each of these aspects but also encompasses the interplay between image and text, including stylistic choices made to rely on one or the other to comport specific information and mood. David B.'s *Epileptic* entails a more complex approach to revealing his brother's neurological experiences than does Keiko Tobe's revelations of her son's autistic world in *With the Light*.[15] Both authors treat serious subjects with depth, gravity, and inspiration and use images to comport information as much as their words do. But the reader must sustain a barrage of stimuli in the former while simply witnessing a report of it in the latter. The requirements made on the reader differ in complexity, although both works demand intellectual and emotional sophistication and strength.

While these two titles share such commonalities as general subject matter (family life with a member whose brain differs from the norm), scope (treatments are explored and described), and format (both are long graphic novels, translated for American readers from different languages), Tobe does not require the reader to experience the condition of autism during the course of her account, while David B. demands that reading his book include the experience of helplessness that a seizure may entail.

Needless to say, there are graphic novel readers for whom complexity is desirable, while there are others for whom this experience of complexity holds little or no interest. The question then is intended to seek the degree of engagement the reader wants from the graphic novel. Should the complexity offered be lifelike or more inferentially demanding?

Where Does the Reader Place Herself?

Because sequential art necessarily offers a concrete point of view, the experienced reader likely knows how that vantage point is best exploited on her behalf. Imperfect parallels to all-text reading include a preference for novels in first person or those with idiomatic speech, or a penchant for omniscient narrators or stream of consciousness exposition. For the sequential art aesthete, as for the dedicated text reader, a preference may be a preference-in-this-moment rather than a dedication that does not sway from week to week, mood to mood, or book to book. But it is a taste component nonetheless: How close does the reader want to be to the action? Does she place herself within the story or prefer to keep a distance?

Visual stimuli offer readers the prospect of becoming more fully engaged in the narrative-as-environment. Think of the difference between seeing a horror movie and reading a straight-text horror novel. While some observers are, of course, more susceptible to visual stimuli, the faculty of sight provides us with unique input from the world. For some graphic novel readers, this stimulation is particularly attractive; for some it may be distracting.

CHILDREN AS SEQUENTIAL ART CONSUMERS

Younger and less experienced readers often have a more difficult time recognizing, let alone discussing, what attributes of their reading have particular and personal appeal. While there are juvenile fans of comics and graphic novels, their ability to analyze their preferences is typically augmented by an older person's providing vocabulary and, typically, unwittingly providing suggested preferences.

Children, as well as older but inexperienced readers, need to read widely in order to find their own tastes. This is no less true with visual literature than with fiction genres. As publishers of mainstream and even curriculum-oriented titles have come to recognize potential economic rewards for graphic novel publishing, children now have the opportunity to find accessible material. Unfortunately, what is available varies in aesthetic quality. Reworking text so that images appear in boxes and words in either balloons or as captions does not a graphic novel make, and including substandard work in the collection and offering it to children during readers' advisory opportunities is likely to teach child readers that graphic novels aren't for them.

There are new efforts to reach children with graphic novel publishing projects that do it very well. Françoise Mouly's new imprint, Toon Books, is a good example of material that has been vetted by both adult creators and child consumers.[16] Rather than reformatting traditional text material, these graphic novels for pre-school-age readers make intrinsic use of the sequential art format.

Children are prone to appreciating—even craving—series. Among aesthetically successful graphic novel series to which both kids and libraries have warmed quickly are Jennifer and Matthew Holm's Babymouse books and Andy Runton's Owly series.[17] Dav Pilkey's very popular Captain Underpants books demonstrate how sequential art and traditional text and illustration components can work together in a single story.[18] Contemporary children are accustomed to cross-media delivery of both information and entertainment, and hybrid graphic novel/illustrated chapter books address this format agnosticism well.

TEEN PREFERENCES

Because so many libraries have accepted graphic novels as a particularly teen-centric literature (in spite of the fact that there is actually nothing age-specific about the format any more than magazines, for example), teens have been granted wider exposure across the past decade than many other American library audiences. However, teens being the most peer-oriented of individuals, many are exposed only to the most popular genres within the format. In one epoch, this has meant that superheroes have prevailed, while now the most ubiquitous option is manga. This means that the teen sequential art lover may not, in fact, have wide experience within the format.

Is it the duty of the readers' advisor to introduce potential readers to materials that aren't on their radar? Of course. Working with teenage graphic novel readers—which today means usually with teen manga readers—takes not only a broad knowledge of what is available, but also a sensitivity to adolescent peer-awareness. With teen clients, the advisor is likely to find greater respect (and usefulness) when he points the teen who is inquiring on a specific subject toward a graphic novel than when he tries to expand the casual manga-reading teen to other sequential art styles worthy of interest. At this point in time, teens see themselves more often as manga readers or as people who do not read manga; introducing a third alternative—sequential art that is not manga—is asking the teen to try something that is other than teen culture. This does not mean that teens can't, won't, or don't like anything but manga; it means that teens are hyperaware that the sequential art they are "supposed" to like (according to their peers) is manga.

ADVISING ADULT ENTHUSIASTS

Moving adult graphic novel readers from titles they know to ones they may want to know calls upon the advisor to understand the individual's tastes, how appeals are perceived by her, and what is available. It is this last necessity that requires the advisor to prepare specifically for the graphic novel enthusiast. A skillful advisor can interview a reader presenting himself with any particular set of appeals and levels of self-awareness about taste. Advisory work generally involves the library's literature collections, the specifics of which the advisor comes to know through both direct reading and reviews, and across a time arc that may be rather long.

Coming to see graphic novels as the purview of all advisors, rather than a niche relegated to a staff member who doesn't carry a robust advisory portfolio, must be the first step in according those in search of reading advice with assistance equal in quality and scale to that accorded mystery fans or biography buffs. Here are some starting points for bringing staff up to the starting line:

- Inventory your library's activities related to general advisory work: who, where, when, how
- Identify collection strengths and weaknesses related to graphic novels: collection plan, collection policies, budget
- Index broader community resources related to graphic novels and readership: which agencies, possible collaborators/competitors
- Analyze current and potential user needs for graphic novel reading advice

WHO SHOULD DO THE WORK?

Being a fan isn't the same as being a professional advisor. But certainly a professional readers' advisor who either eschews graphic novels or actively dislikes them is an unlikely candidate to lead the effort to connect with readers who do like graphic novels and want advice on what to read.

Go with your library's strengths at the outset, but plan to expand those strengths: if current appreciation for the format dwells in a small number of paraprofessional staff, involve them in the professional development of staff who already have the role of providing professional advice.

WHAT'S NEXT . . .

In the following three chapters, we'll discuss graphic novel suggestions related to reading and narrative choices that either have not been informed by prior experience with graphic novels or that can be encouraged on the basis of other format affinities, such as film and games.

Notes

1. John Smylie, "Comics," *The Encyclopedia of Aesthetics*, vol. 1 (New York: Oxford University Press, 1998): 405–9.
2. Susanne K. Langer, *Feeling and Form* (New York: Scribner, 1953).
3. Roland Barthes, *Empire of Signs* (New York: Hill and Wang, 1983) and Barthes' *Image Music Text* (New York: Hill and Wang, 1978), do not directly address comics but observations, queries, and meditations here do address the connections among narrative, image (especially photographic ones), and cultural expectation.
4. Thomas Berger, *Another Way of Telling* (New York: Vintage, 1995).
5. Hergé, The Adventures of Tintin series, beginning with *Tintin in the Land of the Soviets* (San Francisco: Last Gasp, 2003); Marguerite Abouet and Clément Oubrerie, *Aya* (Montreal: Drawn and Quarterly, 2007).
6. Joe Kubert, *Yossel, April 19, 1943: A Story of the Warsaw Ghetto Uprising* (New York: ibooks, 2003); Posy Simmonds, *Tamara Drewe* (Boston: Houghton Mifflin, 2008).
7. Marjane Satrapi, *The Complete Persepolis* (New York: Pantheon, 2007); Ande Parks and Chris Samnee, *Capote in Kansas* (Portland, OR: Oni Press, 2005).
8. Charles Burns, *Black Hole* (New York: Pantheon, 2005); Franz Kafka and Peter Kuper, *Give It Up: And Other Short Stories* (New York: NBM, ComicsLit, 1995).
9. Lewis Trondheim, *Little Nothings: The Curse of the Umbrella* (New York: NBM, ComicsLit, 2008) begins an ongoing series of collections from Trondheim's graphic novel diaries and journals.
10. Ho Che Anderson, *King: A Comics Biography of Martin Luther King, Jr.* (Seattle: Fantagraphics, 2005); Paul Pope, *Heavy Liquid* (New York: DC Comics, Vertigo, 2001).
11. Jason Thomson, *Manga: The Complete Guide* (New York: Ballantine, 2007); Robin Brenner, *Understanding Manga and Anime* (Santa Barbara, CA: Libraries Unlimited, 2007).
12. Adam Sacks, *Salmon Doubts* (Gainesville, FL: Alternative Comics, 2004).
13. Rick Geary, *The Borden Tragedy* (New York: NBM, 1998); Brian Wood and Ryan Kelly, *Local* (Portland, OR: Oni Press, 2008).
14. Sabrina Jones, *Isadora Duncan: A Graphic Biography* (New York: Hill and Wang, 2008); Craig Thompson, *Good-bye, Chunky Rice* (New York: Pantheon, 2006).
15. David B., *Epileptic* (New York: Pantheon, 2005); Keiko Tobe, *With the Light: Raising an Autistic Child* (New York: Yen Press, 2007–2009).

16. Mouly, art editor of *The New Yorker,* contracts with skilled and talented artists and shows their work to classrooms of schoolchildren for their consideration and feedback as a title reaches completion and is readied for publication. She and her husband, noted cartoonist Art Spiegelman, previously published the series Little Lit, which also aimed to provide children with authentic and age-appropriate comics reading experiences.

17. Jennifer Holm and Matthew Holm, *Babymouse: Queen of the World* (New York: Random House, 2005); Andy Runton, *Owly: The Way Home and the Bittersweet Summer* (Marietta, GA: Top Shelf Productions, 2004). Both titles have developed into ongoing series; the former is published by a mainstream publisher and the latter by a sequential art one.

18. Dav Pilkey, *The Adventures of Captain Underpants* (New York: Blue Sky Press, 1997). There have been a variety of sequels to, reissues of, and repackaging of this title.

4
MOVING TRADITIONAL READERS TOWARD GRAPHIC NOVEL OPTIONS

In the previous chapter, we considered the needs of graphic novel readers who want to find guidance as they select new graphic novels. In this chapter, we will discuss the needs and concerns of, and best practices associated with, readers who have not yet had their interest piqued by sequential art.

Readers read and advisors advise. One of the delights of performing readers' advisory work is enabling readers to find options they weren't able to find unassisted. There are more readers, of all ages, who *don't* read graphic novels than there are graphic novel readers; that's true in the United States, although not in Japan. And for readers in some age groups in some cultures, the numbers game might come a lot closer to parity than here.

Why would you want to steer a reader toward graphic novels? Certainly the format isn't one that every reader may find intuitively comfortable. But the fact is that many readers have never explored the format due to simple prejudice, and part of what we do as librarians is offer lifelong learning opportunities—including the opportunity to reconsider decisions readers may have made about what's a "good" book.

OLD SAWS STILL ALIVE AND GRINDING

While children are more open to new formats and, today, are likely to be format-agnostic when it comes to media that include reading options, adults of a certain age grew up during an era when comics were frowned upon.[1] While many of these adults aren't consciously hostile toward sequential art, the format simply isn't on their radar, or if it is, the perceived wisdom continues that "comics are for kids." With the boom of graphic novels targeting the teen market in consumer and library forums, adults may also believe that the appeal of comics is adolescent, a judgment unlikely to pique mature adult interest.

As the publishing world becomes increasingly cross-cultural and format-rich, ignoring consideration of graphic novels for such a reader is unfair both to that reader and to culture as an evolving, living thing. While *individuals* may be disinclined to read more than one or two graphic novels, our audience as a whole needs to have the option brought to their attention.

BRINGING GRAPHIC NOVELS INTO THE READERS' ADVISOR'S PURVIEW

Readers are best served by advisors who do not allow their own literary prejudices and tastes to control their advising. Clearly, every advisor has his or her favorite—and unfavorite—reading options. But in order to provide excellent service to readers, the advisor must know a breadth of genres, tastes, and cultural relevancies. As I work with a reader who knows he likes romance fiction, has read widely in it, and also recognizes his own interest in accurate period detail, I need to consider options to suggest that take him to books he wants to read, not where *I* (no fan of romance fiction in my personal reading life) believe *he* could better spend his time.

In order to do that, I must read widely and liberally, becoming familiar with the books and tastes of the moment as well as deepening my knowledge of canonical authors and publishing houses in a wide array of genres and taste areas. Graphic novels are books, so they deserve to be included in this background from which I can serve advice capably and comprehensively.

INTRODUCING A FORMAT

The good readers' advisor always offers choices rather than directing her client to a title with the promise that this is the absolute best selection. By including an appropriate graphic novel among the handful of proffered suggestions, the advisor opens the way for a conversation about how the format may be a satisfying discovery for this particular reader at this particular time. It is through that conversation and, optimally, a shared viewing of a passage from a graphic novel that the uninitiated reader may begin to consider the format as a possible avenue for reading exploration.

As with any reading advice, the advisor should have some certainty about what the proffered graphic novel entails, not only in terms of genre and basic appeals, but also suitability to this reader's taste for degree of difficulty, sensibilities about propriety, and desires for intellectual rigor. Just as you wouldn't advise someone about a good movie without clear awareness of how well a particular film's style fits the expectations and limitations of the viewer, don't offer a graphic novel just because it is one.

How to Include the Format

Once you've decided to include the format when working with readers who haven't considered graphic novels, be sure you've done your homework before you offer specific suggestions. This includes building your sense of familiarity with the format, its genres and stylistic considerations such as detailed depictions in image as well as text. See appendix A if you are just as much a non–graphic novel reader as the clients you plan to bring to the format. From there, follow the suggestions below when working with a reader new to the format:

Conduct your typical readers' advisory interview, garnering insight into the reader's tastes, immediate needs, reading values or hopes, and reading history.

Inquire about the reader's interest in nontext narrative formats, such as favorite movies.

Work with the reader at the catalog or the bookshelf, as you would ordinarily, collecting three to five titles for brief booktalking.

Include a graphic novel suitable to the details collected in the interview.

Provide the reader with the opportunity to consider the narrative style of each of your suggestions, appraising whether the sample offers a satisfying reading experience in its vocabulary, syntax, and rhetorical details.

Provide a brief reason for including the graphic novel, such as its fit with the reader's preferred genre, political or social interests, and the stellar aspects of its narrative workings, such as its use of color as symbolism or detailed re-creation of a time period.

Show the reader an example of what you are describing by sharing a page spread and pointing out visual details.

Expect Concerns about Ability

Often, adult readers who have not read extended sequential art pieces express doubt about their ability to track panels. This belief seems to arise from the typical reluctance many of us harbor about trying something new, and our willingness to excuse ourselves based on an element we can see as heterogeneous to our previous experiences. Have you ever heard someone excuse himself from tasting an exotic food, one whose flavor and texture he may have no experience with, using the excuse that he knows he won't like it because he doesn't like (fill in the food group)? It is easy enough to look at calamari rings and say: "I won't like them because I don't like fish, based on my experience with canned tuna." Easy, yes; but informed, no.

How do you respond to such a dismissal? Being a readers' advisor regularly requires both tact and a sensitivity to knowing when to push and when to let go of a suggestion now and repeat it at another juncture. Maybe the most that will happen during this first attempt with this particular reader is that you have made her aware that such a format is in the collection, that you, the advisor, respect its possibilities, and that you are available to consult in the future about formats beyond her usual reading experience.

With reading, there is the added issue of doubting one's ability to learn how to strip meaning from print in a way previously untested by the reader: "I can't read that because the panels will confuse me. I won't know what to do first."

Therefore, be prepared to show the reader how to track the page, reassuring her that she can become accustomed to it within a couple of pages. Don't suggest that "it's so easy, you'll have no problem doing it." Allow her to doubt, but show her the simplicity of taking steps to get beyond that doubt.

CROSSING OVER

The best place to start with graphic novel suggestions for adult readers who haven't read inside this format may be from the collection of sequential art titles that reviewers describe as having crossover potential. Certainly, if you, as a readers' advisor, lack familiarity with the format, the crossover books should be added to your own reading list.

Crossover graphic novels are those that offer strong narrative lines along with thorough character and/or plot development. In short, they are graphic novels that align well with appeal categories that are popular among readers of narrative fiction and nonfiction. They are not illustrated novels; graphic novels, as we noted in the opening chapter of this book and as has been noted widely throughout the literature, are created with interconnecting image and text relying on constant feedback and symbiosis with each other.[2]

Many crossover selections are genre-oriented. Genre allegiance is part of the reader appeal that opens the graphic novel to possible interest and engagement by the novice graphic novel reader. The following suggestions offer some genre-strong graphic novels that offer familiar genre tropes for the new graphic novel reader.

Short Stories

A small step may be helpful to some readers unsure about sampling a format that is relatively unknown to them. Whether they read all of the stories in either of these collections or just sample one or two, they'll get a good feel for why graphic novel literature offers readers something different from text-only literature, film, or other narrative-carrying media.

House of Java by Mark Murphy is peopled by characters visiting—or not—a coffee shop that is pretty much on a route between here and there without being in an exciting place of its own.[3] That's fine, because these are character-driven, realistic stories featuring adults suffering from nothing more shocking than anomie, depression, or niggling suspicion and nothing more bizarre than eagerness. Clear black-and-white images, with little shading, are easy on the eye while offering first-time graphic novel readers details that are meaningful.

Jamilti and Other Stories by Rutu Modan also offers a variety of stories focused on relationships, with the settings varied among contemporary Palestine and a not-quite-folkloric Europe.[4] The full-color art depicts the various locations with details that communicate climate as well as manufactured objects; the individuals are clearly distinguishable and realistically homely. Many of these stories have a political edge that offers easy access to readers interested in contemporary world affairs.

Mystery and Crime

Murder mysteries come in a wide range of subgenre specialties, including cozies, hard-boiled, police procedurals, and those featuring amateur sleuths. Devotees of mystery and detective novels are likely to have a preference among these subgenres but, in the main, are attracted to reading about human relationships, considering puzzles, and investigating appearances with an awareness that something beyond mere appearances informs reality.

Some excellent crossover graphic novels for mystery and detection buffs include

Miss Don't Touch Me by Hubert and Kerascoet provides all the characterization, setting, and atmosphere of Elizabeth George.[5] Set during the Jazz Age in Paris, a young woman seeks to find her sister's killers. In the process, she goes to work in an upscale brothel, but her work there is not conveyed as titillating. Much of the period detail and emotional lives of the characters are conveyed through the images, making this a fine example of the graphic novel format, while the plot and its development speak well to traditional mystery lovers.

Capote in Kansas by Ande Parks and Chris Samnee recapitulates the research Truman Capote undertook as he worked to create *In Cold Blood.*[6] While there is no mystery about who slaughtered the murder victims, mystery readers interested in what makes criminals tick— and/or what makes writers write about murder—are offered much to ponder and explore here. The use of color, light, and shadow in the visual elements provides new graphic novel readers with the beginnings of a visual vocabulary that can aid them in reading less narrative-driven sequential art.

The Borden Tragedy by Rick Geary is one in a successful series of true crime studies by a cartoon journalist.[7] Geary reports both the facts and the suspicions surrounding the Lizzie Borden affair through a visual lens that forces the reader into its nineteenth-century world. The sequential art includes diagrams and the volume includes a bibliography for further exploration of this American legend. Many mystery readers have a penchant for series, so this, too, offers the possibility of starting a new cycle of such reading.

Science Fiction and Fantasy

While many graphic novels, including lots of manga and most superhero stories, belong to these related genres, the selection of those that allow the neophyte graphic novel taster access is neither broad nor deep. Compelling narratives that include high production values enable the new reader to readily see the relevance of images as part of the narrative flow and feel.

Among the many graphic novels in these genres that provide such access are

Heavy Liquid by Paul Pope has an only slightly future urban setting, noir undercurrent, and imaginative invention of a material that offers value to artists and drug traders.[8] There's a punk sensibility in the drawing style and color is used to highlight scenes of social upheaval, personal threat, and brave aesthetic experiment. As attractive to devotees of urban fiction as to those with steampunk interests, this one offers no masks or superhero tights, just realistic people in a grim new world.

Cairo by G. Willow Wilson and M. K. Perker is fantasy-lite just as *Heavy Liquid* is sci-fi-lite, but just as smooth an introductory point for non–graphic novel readers.[9] Diverse characters run around the modern Egyptian city and collide with one another. They include a deracinated American, a drug smuggler, an Israeli soldier, and a journalist. There is a magician whose skills threaten to wreak havoc—or save the others from themselves and their confrontations. The painterly art is smooth and clearly detailed, pulling the reader's eye into the backgrounds as well as the foregrounds of nearly every panel.

Charles Dixon and David Wenzel's adaptation of J. R. R. Tolkien's *The Hobbit* may surprise purists of the original.[10] Here's an excellent example of how sequential art interpretation extends the reader's imagination rather than intruding upon it.

Romance

Many of the manga titles on offer in the West are romantic comedies. New graphic novel readers may think this is all that the format has to offer, and since marketing tends to push the options most attractive to teen consumers to the front, adult readers unfamiliar with graphic novels may have dismissed the format's ability to portray romance in a meaningful, adult manner.

Of course, there are lots of manga titles that address adult romantic interests, but the larger format of comics may be introduced more efficiently to new graphic novel readers through stories that are more contained than a long-running series.

Depending on the generation of your new graphic novels reader, you might suggest one of these:

Ethel and Ernest by Raymond Briggs is actually a biography of the artist's parents.[11] But it's a romantic story in the quietest, most accessible of ways. Briggs's tiny panels and soft palette complement the working-class history of his folks, whose lives encompassed both world wars and the evolution of milk delivery from horse-drawn cart to truck to supermarket shelf. These are real people, lovingly restored to life by their son.

Blue Pills by Frederik Peeters tells a finely balanced love story involving a young—and somewhat hedonistic—man, an HIV-positive single mother, and her toddler.[12] Over the course of the story they not only find love, but make a happy home together. The expressive black-and-white art provides quick and thorough characterizations and tracks changes in mood.

Tamara Drewe by Posy Simmonds shows, rather than tells, readers about the lust, jealousy, and self-centeredness of romance, as well as revealing the reliance that infatuated people have on maintaining a safe distance from flaw-revealing reality.[13] With roots in Thomas Hardy's characterizations, Simmonds's storytelling perfectly interweaves image and word, allowing each to bear its full weight and strength. This romance doesn't end with a happily ever after, but it does offer insight on the human condition that includes ill-fated efforts to gain love.

Suspense and Thriller

While this genre is richly represented in fine—and not so fine—graphic novels, it's tricky to identify ones that have crossover appeal for readers to whom the format is not a known or understood quantity. You might want to help your new graphic novel reader by offering something that isn't visually overwhelming in its graphic presentation of gore, perhaps (but this could be a draw, so conduct that ever-important reference interview), and that treats the ability to suspend disbelief with both respect and authority.

You might start with one of these:

Exit Wounds by Rutu Modan is peopled with characters who seem straight-forward and ingenuous but are actually politically complex and emotionally conniving: a young Israeli cab driver, the woman who calls him out of the blue to announce his father's death in a bombing, and, importantly, the estranged father, who may—or may not—have been at the scene where his scarf was found after the bombing.[14] Clear line art captures the urban and rural scenery, as well as the young adults' skeptical expressions and postures.

Elk's Run by Joshua Hale Fialkov, Noel Tuazon, and Scott A. Keating is, in some ways, a stereotypical guns-and-ammo suspense tale with a twist.[15] But for first-time graphic novel readers, it offers an excellent bridge because the storytellers employ stylistic changes in the art to portray important motivating memories held by the main characters. *Elk's Run* is a place that the adult, right-wing inhabitants hope that time and the authorities forgot, but their militaristic protection is broken when their kids become more dynamic thinkers.

Historical Fiction

Historical fiction offers readers plot and characterization but also appropriate period scenery and social systems. The graphic novel can depict any or all of these attributes.

You might suggest to the historical fiction buff one or more of these:

Bourbon Island 1730 by Lewis Trondheim and Olivier Appollodorus is a complex and engaging pirate story told with the same rhythms and authority as Robert Louis Stevenson.[16] Because Trondheim includes his hallmark characterizations of individuals by giving each the appearance of the bird or animal that his or her personality seems to be like (for instance, the timid man having the head of a chicken), the new graphic novel reader will have good cause and much encouragement to attend to the details of the images, while following a plot that is well-researched and adventurous.

A Jew in Communist Prague by Vittorio Giardino is a five-part novel and only the first three are available in English.[17] While this is frustrating to those who are submersed in the story's arc, it can also serve to demonstrate the compelling nature of the well-told graphic novel. Told from the viewpoint of the mature teenaged son of a couple who have been split by the father's arrest, the generously sized, full-color pages show details of the setting, clothing, and social strata that existed in 1950s Eastern Europe. The text is precise, modest, and powerful.

Usagi Yojimbo by Stan Sakai is a long-running manga series featuring samurai rabbits.[18] Each volume is self-contained and substantive enough to be satisfying on its own. And each provides credible and engaging historical detail as well as satisfying plotting and characterizations of the feudal Japanese protagonists.

Mythology and Science: Mirrors of Our Daily Lives

These literary niches straddle creative fiction and the realms of history, sociology, religion, and psychology. The graphic novel format is particularly well-suited as a vehicle for giving readers entrée to classical mythology and popular science, whether readers bring a thorough grounding in more traditional works or are just beginning to explore cultural narrative artifacts.

Eric Shanower's Age of Bronze series retells the story of the Trojan War with well-researched imagery and attention to narrative detail.[19] In keeping with authentic recorded mythology, the watershed events in the lives of gods and demigods in the associated tales are not presented in strict chronological order, but rather in the most pertinent sequence for the overall tale to unfold. Shanower includes lists of his source material, so serious researchers can go from his work to its foundations in classical scholarship.

Referencing another basic resource, and providing a quantity of scientific information as well, neurobiologist Jay Hosler's *Clan Apis* presents the role of myth in civilization while showing how honeybee colonies maintain a role in environmental science.[20] While often marketed for classroom use, this story of one honeybee's life cycle can engage readers through adults. The clear, black-and-white cartoons and generous font may be less daunting to some older readers who fear that sequential art's very layout will confuse them.

War and Politics

Readers with sophisticated tastes in narrative nonfiction may be surprised that the graphic novel vehicle can provide viewpoints on politics and other current affairs that are rich, unique, and provocative. When offering a crossover title to the traditional reader with a taste for serious nonfiction, be sure to communicate the essential additive qualities these books offer, rather than presenting them as alternatives to other, likely traditionally written, texts:

Joe Sacco's *Safe Area Gorazde* demands the reader bring a knowledge of late twentieth-century European history and an interest in journalism as a business—or at least be willing to consider these concepts.[21] Sacco provides compelling observations, analyses, and questions about life in Bosnia during the years of recent internecine warfare and U.N. presence. In light of even more recent "embedded journalism" realities in the Middle East, his portrayal of his informers and of himself as one who didn't simply interview and observe, but socialized with combatants, civilians, and victims of warfare, is trenchant. Sacco's black-and-white art is as essential to his reports as the text he supplies to quote these informers or describe motivations and events as he learns of them.

Keiji Nakazawa's *Barefoot Gen* is a classic; the publication of the English translation in the United States predates popular interest in manga.[22] It reveals the physical, environmental, social, spiritual, and political effects of the atom bombing of Hiroshima. This is a culturally appropriate way to read about the on-the-ground experiences of civilians, through a lens that was about thirty years from the historic event when authored. Offering it to contemporary readers who think of manga only as romances collected by teens is a sure way to show them the difference between a format's possibilities and the instances by which they may have judged it.

Stuck Rubber Baby by Howard Cruse is a fictionalized but authentic account of how growing up gay in the South during the Civil Rights Era can shape an Everyman.[23] Readers looking for genuinely informed books about either gay culture or experience, outsiders, the South in the early 1960s, or the nexus of these social forces can be offered this, with attention drawn to the evocative and beautiful art that is essential to the narrative's unfolding.

Rather than feeling limited to the titles suggested here, I hope you can add your own discoveries of crossovers that resonate with adult readers who have defined tastes and reading desires, but who are novices in graphic novel reading. The list above is meant to be incentive, rather than prescriptive.

RECONNECT AND CRITIQUE YOUR ADVICE

When you do place a graphic novel successfully into the hands of a new sequential art reader, be sure to follow up on the reader's next visit, by asking how that initial reading experience went. Did she find the book a pleasure? Or did she struggle but ultimately find herself glad to have access to its narrative content? Was your suggestion on the mark in terms of connecting the right story with this reader?

Especially if you are new at giving graphic novel reading advice, you may want to ask more analytical questions of your first novice readers; but remember, you are now analyzing your own effectiveness, not grilling the reader about her experiences.

Listen to the feedback your first-time graphic novel reader offers. She may put forward appeal ideas that hadn't occurred to you, especially if you are a longtime reader of the format. Utilize the fresh eyes to inform your own advising vocabulary and sensitivities.

And be prepared to hear that the reader didn't actually get around to reading the graphic novel at all, that she took it because you were nice enough to suggest it but that, on her own, it just didn't rise to the top of her reading stack before the due date. If the reader is open to it—and you'll know if she isn't—try an alternative suggestion in your next encounter. Acknowledge that your first suggestion might not have been engaging enough (*enough* being a measure of what gets her nose in the book, not a judgment of your expertise as an advisor), but note that there are other possibilities that very well might engage.

WHEN NOT TO PUSH AND WHEN TO PROD A BIT

Don't push the adult reader who is adamant about dismissing sequential art as a viable personal reading option. On the other hand, keep your advisory session educational, noting that the format does indeed have something to offer some readers. You might suggest that he consider whether he'd want to read a particular title in order to discuss it with his child, partner, or other graphic novel–reading acquaintance.

The mythology about comics and juvenile readership may lead you to assume that graphic novels are a necessary component when advising some reading teens. Not all teens are manga fans, and some inveterate readers in that age group dismiss sequential art, in part to rebel against being seen as just another member of the popular culture pack. Do push a bit with such teen readers, rather than allow them to miss out on some very fine reading material. Don't suggest that they read a particular graphic novel because all their peers are reading it—or because none of their peers are. Suggest a book on its own merits, in conjunction with this teen reader's tastes, rather than packaging the advice as social advice.

WORKING WITH GROUPS

One excellent way to introduce readers to a book format previously unexplored by most of them is to include a graphic novel in a standing book discussion program or as a companion in a film program. In these cases, you are working with a group of readers—or viewers—and need to consider group dynamics as well as appeal details. Before selecting a graphic novel to include in a group situation, consider these questions, in order:

- What brings this group together around books (or films)?
- What's the previous experience of the group with the medium around which they coalesce?
- Is there a graphic novel advocate (or two or three) in the group?
- Looking ahead to the titles you plan to consider in the next several sessions of the group's meeting, which title, or topic, suggests a good opportunity for including a graphic novel?
- Is there an accessible graphic novel available in sufficient numbers of copies to satisfy the group's needs?

By considering the purpose of the group and the personal reasons its members participate in it, you will be able to focus on the type of graphic novel that might be most appropriate, either by genre or subject or by degree of difficulty or accessibility. Some such groups are populated by experienced readers (or viewers) who know each other well and have met together long enough to know each other's prejudices, whether or not they are clear about their own. Certainly, the presence of members who read and appreciate the medium you want to introduce to the group can serve to assist the introduction. However, it's possible to introduce graphic novels to a group in which no one is a current aficionado. Your introduction will, in the latter case, be entirely up to you, while in the former you can present the new format with the assistance of those for whom it is already familiar.

Several states maintain a Center for the Book, which you may find an excellent resource, either for book discussion materials or suggestions of graphic novels that are "book discussion-able."[24]

When working with film discussion groups, you may find as much reluctance to discuss a book as you do to discuss a graphic novel in particular. Or not! Don't assume that your group audience will be negative about graphic novels just because they have coalesced around a related but not identical affinity medium. An easy starting point with a film group would be, of course, to select a graphic novel on which a film has been based.[25]

TAKING YOUR EFFORT TO A REALLY BIG CROWD

Many communities in the United States have developed "one book" experiences in the past decade. These efforts may involve the sophisticated approach highlighting grant winners of the National Endowment for the Arts programs, or they may be grassroots and modest.[26] Such initiatives aim to involve the local community in a shared experience with a specific book, to build community, promote literacy, and act as a catalyst for public dialogue about issues on which the selected title touches. Often, copies of the selected book are provided through giveaways, and events are staged across a period of time so that readers may come together to explore aspects of their experiences with the book.

Some communities have already broken ground in making that shared reading experience be one of examining a graphic novel.[27] This can be most successful, in terms of bringing new readers to the format, if the community has experienced previous "one city, one book" programs and has bought into the "unity through reading" ethos these programs inspire. Such ambitious projects require the general population to trust that the book being proffered is worthwhile and, having agreed to that premise on earlier occasions, the mass audience is more likely to give the graphic novel round a shot.

For such large-scale "advising," your selection of a graphic novel needs to take into account all the issues that any book selection for a community-wide read must address, including the attraction and appropriateness of the title to a general population and relevant programming that can be spun from mass reading of the selected title. In this situation, the readers' advisor must know and understand the community at large, rather than work with specific individuals within it. What sort of narrative would be relevant here and now, in this community? And why a graphic novel? These questions are important to answer before wading into the launch of determining that the "right" book is a graphic novel.

There are also times and places where something smaller scaled than a full-on citywide read might be a good entry point for the advisor who is ready to introduce the format to a broad audience. Some school districts sponsor school-based community reads; or you, as a readers' advisor, may be asked to share some reading suggestions on local radio. While there may be less fanfare around such broad announcing of a good graphic novel for many to read, either of these announcement venues can bring new readers to the format by introducing them to one title you've carefully selected as best to share with many, and probably mostly unknown, participants.

WHAT'S NEXT . . .

In the next chapter, we examine tie-ins between graphic novels and other narrative media, including television, film, and games. Such tie-ins offer the advisor entry possibilities for bringing graphic novels to the attention of both confirmed and ingénue readers. In the case of the advisor selecting a single title to offer to a broad audience, this may be the best starting place when determining a graphic novel that can be shown as accessible and appealing to many.

Notes

1. The golden age of comic books, a medium that attracted readers of all ages in the United States during the second quarter of the twentieth century, was brought to a dramatic close in 1954, when noted psychiatrist Fredric Wertham published a poorly conducted study that seemed to tie comics reading to juvenile delinquency. *Seduction of the Innocent* (most recently republished by Main Street Books in 1996) gained traction in such venues as PTA groups, and led to enforced reforms in comics publishing and a demise of the variegated and rich texture of genres, appeals, and accessibility of comics. See an overview of the social history of comics, sequential art, and graphic novel publishing in my *Graphic Novels Now* (Chicago: American Library Association, 2005).
2. Art Spiegelman describes the interaction between image and word in the format as emulating thinking itself, which includes our moving between mental images and utilizing word-concepts: "[O]ne of the reasons comics are effective is that they mimic the way the brain works. One doesn't think in holograms of reality . . . You remember . . . on the basis of very abstracted information rather than a three-dimensional film . . . Cartoon drawing does that . . . The words [work] similarly. One doesn't think in complete sentences but in small bursts of language." See his description of the image/word/reader interaction in "What Comics Do When They Do It Right" (*Voice of Youth Advocates* 25 (2002): 360–62).
3. Mark Murphy, *House of Java*, 2 vols. (New York: NBM, ComicsLit, 1998, 2002).
4. Rutu Modan, *Jamilti and Other Stories* (Montreal: Drawn and Quarterly, 2008).
5. Hubert and Kerascoet, *Miss Don't Touch Me* (New York: NBM, ComicsLit, 2008).
6. Ande Parks and Chris Samnee, *Capote in Kansas* (Portland, OR: Oni Press, 2005).
7. Rick Geary, *The Borden Tragedy* (New York: NBM, 1998).
8. Paul Pope, *Heavy Liquid* (New York: DC Comics, Vertigo, 2001).
9. G. Willow Wilson and M. K. Perker, *Cairo* (New York: DC Comics, Vertigo, 2007).
10. Charles Dixon, David Wenzel, and J. R. R. Tolkien, *The Hobbit: An Illustrated Edition of the Fantasy Classic* (New York: Ballantine, 1990).

11. Raymond Briggs, *Ethel and Ernest: A True Story* (New York: Knopf, 1999).
12. Frederik Peeters, *Blue Pills: A Positive Love Story* (Boston: Houghton Mifflin, 2008).
13. Posy Simmonds, *Tamara Drewe* (Boston: Houghton Mifflin, 2008).
14. Rutu Modan, *Exit Wounds* (Montreal: Drawn and Quarterly, 2007).
15. Joshua Hale Fialkov, Noel Tuazon, and Scott A. Keating, *Elk's Run* (New York: Villard, 2007).
16. Lewis Trondheim and Olivier Appollodorus, *Bourbon Island 1730* (New York: First Second Books, 2008).
17. Vittorio Giardino, *A Jew in Communist Prague* (New York: NBM, ComicsLit, 1997–).
18. Stan Sakai, *Usagi Yojimbo* (Seattle: Fantagraphics, 1984–).
19. Eric Shanower, Age of Bronze (Berkeley, CA: Image Comics, 2001–).
20. Jay Hosler, *Clan Apis* (Columbus, OH: Active Synapse, 2000).
21. Joe Sacco, *Safe Area Gorazde: The War in Eastern Bosnia, 1992–1995* (Seattle: Fantagraphics, 2000).
22. Keiji Nakazawa, *Barefoot Gen* (San Francisco: Last Gasp, 2004–2009).
23. Howard Cruse, *Stuck Rubber Baby* (New York: Paradox Press, 1995).
24. While the California Center for the Book actually circulates a collection of graphic novels for library discussion groups to use, other such centers provide suggestions online or expand on the authors whom they feature by listing graphic novels to which they have contributed.
25. See chapter 5 for a brief list of such graphic novels and, more helpfully, tools for discovering more.
26. The National Endowment for the Arts' "Big Read" program has helped communities to underwrite shared reading experiences with readers' guides, posters, and programming ideas to aid the development of local initiatives centered around any of about three dozen selected titles. "One City, One Book" models have been undertaken in many cities and smaller towns without such elaborate funding or augmenting materials: Chicago, Seattle, San Francisco, and other places have been involved in such initiatives for nearly ten years. See the Library of Congress's Center for the Book at www.loc.gov/loc/cfbook/ for a database of such initiatives that is searchable by location and by book.
27. In 2006, the Seattle Public Library sponsored a "Seattle Reads" initiative centered on Marjane Satrapi's *Persepolis: The Story of a Childhood* (Pantheon, 2003), while in 2007 the city of Edinburgh, Scotland, was the site of a mass giveaway of 25,000 copies of Robert Louis Stevenson's *Kidnapped* in various editions that included a graphic novel by Alan Grant and Cam Kennedy.

5

MOVING BETWEEN GRAPHIC NOVELS AND MEDIA, BETWEEN MEDIA AND GRAPHIC NOVELS

In the previous chapter, we considered the needs of readers who want to find guidance as they select new graphic novels. In this chapter, we will discuss the needs and concerns of, and best practices associated with, advising between media interests.

Sequential art realizes some traits shared by some nonprint media; those who appreciate film, whether live-action or animated, may well appreciate graphic novel narratives as well. Image and action are components of both the graphic novel format and the film format. Accessing the narrative, in both cases, calls upon the viewer to participate to the degree that images are retained as she advances through the story. In both formats, characterizations rely on visual components and on the audience's awareness and/or knowledge of symbolism such as color choice, facial expression, posture, and background scenery.

WHAT LIMITS THE ADVISOR?

While the traditional readers' advisor works within the confines of printed texts, many libraries today offer advisory tools and services geared to users who want to explore multimedia collections. Websites and in-house lists of subject- or award-specific movies, opera recordings, and other nonprint works are not unusual finds, especially in urban public libraries. The largest American libraries—as well as some smaller and nimble ones—are producing and presenting their own podcasts of locally held programs.

Such portals to the collections do, in fact, provide advice to users; they point the way for those looking for more of whatever it is that they already find worthwhile. And isn't this the whole point of offering readers' advisory services: to give the individual user guidance, when wanted, for making future selections, based on awareness of taste, the history of one's exposure to ideas to date, and the availability of material that suits the criteria that can be limned between these?

As library collections continue to diversify in their formats, advising across formats becomes increasingly necessary. For over a decade, librarians have attempted to assist students with homework assignments that have been written in a manner that forces the student (and librarian) to select material based on format, rather than relevancy of content. We have been frustrated by this blind loyalty to format.[1] Imagine learning to drive from a handbook that is text only. Imagine learning to drive from a video. Now imagine learning from a video game, which one participates in rather than viewing passively. There are choices to offer, and the credible readers' advisor evaluates format for its relevance to the individual as well as content.

DIFFERENCES BETWEEN VIEWING AND READING

Viewing Daniel Clowes's *Ghost World* offers a different aesthetic, cerebral, and physical experience than does reading the book. The narrative outline is the same. Due to fine casting choices, the characters look very much the same. Of course, we do not actually hear the words spoken in the graphic novel, except in our mind's ear. But we also do not actually see the movements: we don't know if, in the words of Jerry Seinfeld, one character or another is a slow talker. We don't have access to anyone's gait.

These do not essentially change the story if we are familiar with it in both these formats. However, if we have been exposed only to the film version, on what merit might we profit by reading the graphic novel? Or, conversely, having read the book, what's the point of seeing the movie?

These are issues for the readers' advisor to consider when working in a milieu where multiple formats are not only possible, but likely to be within the range of the reader before her.

One large distinction between the graphic novel and the movie is that the reader can move backward and forward, trace along the path of one character or another by picking him from the full text on this page and that. The movie viewer, especially if she is alone and has a decent remote control device, can also stop the film, jump from scene to scene, but with less flexibility than the reader, and always with more forethought. A reader can browse while a movie viewer must be more firmly locked into the single moment currently passing before her eyes.

ADVISING THE READER ON MOVIES

It's unlikely that a reader needs to hear a suggestion that he see the movie after having read the book. At least, it's unlikely that such advice needs the careful thinking and planning that should be the forte of the professional readers' advisor. Instead, this might be off-the-cuff advice, passed from neighbor or friend. Instead, finding the beneath-the-surface markers that suggest similarities of style, subject, attitude, attention to visual and narrative symbolism, and cadence are the values an advisor can provide.

For example, *Ghost World,* both the film and the book, share similar stylistic features. But there are other movies that the *Ghost World* reader may find consonant with her reading experience:

> *SubUrbia* presents a similar combination of slacker ennui and artistic drive from its main characters.

> *Art School Confidential* shares parentage, by way of another Clowes book (*Eightball*) and movie direction by Terry Zwigoff, with *Ghost World.*[2]

> *Waking Life*'s technology offers the viewer both live action and cartoon interpolation, a melding that will feel familiar with those who view live-action movies based on drawn narratives.

WHERE TO FIND HELP

The readers' advisor who is aware of graphic novel appeal categories and the specific titles in his collection can begin to grow his awareness of relevant stories in other media to suggest to the dedicated graphic novel reader. Among the most useful tools for exploring such possibilities are

> All Movie Guide (www.allmovie.com) is the portal to movie information on an international level, including synopses, authors, remakes, and related formats.

> Rotten Tomatoes Guide to Best Animated Films (www.rottentomatoes .com/guides/best_animated_films/) is a list of fifty that includes some juvenile titles, but also ranges through full-length features created with an adult audience in mind. Each synopsis provides comparative descriptors of story, art, theme, and content.

AND WHAT TO DO WITH THESE TOOLS

First, having a database of movies is, by itself, no more valuable to your advice seeker than knowing that maybe she would like to enhance her appreciation for graphic novels by selecting a movie to watch. These are the mere beginning points. As this reader's advisor, you must bring some value to the interaction between these possibilities.

One aspect of that value requires prep work: you need to know graphic novels and you need to know movies. You don't need to be familiar with *everything* in either format, of course, but you do need to have a developed frame of reference that will allow you to see the similar and possible appeals between specifics in these formats.

Track your reading and your viewing. Look for common appeal markers. Listen to how others discuss both their reading (of graphic novels) and their movie watching. These steps are no different from ones you would take in refining your general readers' advisory skills. But you will need to hone in on the specific formats, both as a consumer and as an observer.

To help you start your own log of cross-format recommendations, some examples are presented in table 5.1. Don't just memorize these examples, but use them as models to create your own. These examples necessarily look back from a given point in publishing and production time. You'll need to consider books and movies that come along in the future. And because you are moving between formats, that future may include a new book that can be related to an old movie and vice versa.

CINEMATIC ARTS AREN'T JUST MOVIES: THE SMALL SCREEN

A format sometimes ignored by readers' advisors when they are searching for narrative familiarity on which to base a discussion of appeals is television. With the broadening of what was once a relatively narrow broadcast market to include hundreds of channels and the availability of past series as prepackaged sets, the advisor should look to the medium as relevant within advisory discussions.

When faced with an advice seeker who is conversant about television series, be ready to draw advisory parallels to graphic novels. Again, like movies and books, this doesn't mean that you need to have personal experience viewing every episode of every series, but rather that you know

Table 5.1
Cross-Format Recommendations

GRAPHIC NOVEL	FILM	COMMON APPEAL CHARACTERISTICS	DIFFERENCES (BEYOND FORMAT!)
Eric Drooker's *Flood!*[a]	Peter Weir's *The Last Wave*	• Visually centered and rich • Metaphor of water • Urban setting	• Graphic novel contains no text, while film uses typical dialogue and music • Graphic novel's story is benign, while film has thriller and psychic elements
Eric Drooker's *Blood Song*[b]	Ray C. Smallwood's *Camille* with Rudolph Valentino	• No dialogue is available to the viewer • Romance at heart of narrative • Theme of woman trying to start over • Urban setting	• Graphic novel protagonist is Asian woman in Western country, while film's characters are all European • Male interest in film is portrayed as successful member of society, while graphic novel's is an outsider musician
Ande Parks and Chris Samnee's *Capote in Kansas*[c]	Bennett Miller's *Capote*	• Depiction of Truman Capote's time spent researching *In Cold Blood* • Realistic portrayals of individuals involved, both physically and using quotations from primary sources	• Graphic novel explores Capote's relationship with fellow author and co-researcher Harper Lee in some depth while the movie concentrates on the relationship between Capote and Perry, one of the murderers he is researching • Graphic novel's use of monochromes provide color symbolism, while movie's realism extends to naturalistic scene lighting and full color

GRAPHIC NOVEL	FILM	COMMON APPEAL CHARACTERISTICS	DIFFERENCES (BEYOND FORMAT!)
Steven Weissman's *White Flower Day*[d]	Hal Roach's Our Gang and other Little Rascals shorts	• Episodic slapstick featuring children, but from an adult perspective • Caricature rather than character development	• Graphic novel's characters are supernatural, while movie features essentially realistic kids • Little Rascals stories portray traditional ethics and developing consciences in child characters, while graphic novel offers amoral plot developments

[a] Eric Drooker, *Flood!* (Dark Horse, 2002).
[b] Eric Drooker, *Blood Song* (Harcourt, 2002).
[c] Ande Parks and Chris Samnee, *Capote in Kansas* (Oni Press, 2005).
[d] Steven Weissman, *White Flower Day* (Fantagraphics, 2003).

how to find out essential appeal categories that address specific series. Here are some tools to help you analyze television options:

BBC America (www.bbcamerica.com/shows_az.jsp). Story arcs, characters, and brief samples of shows, when taken together, provide a variety of appeal categories to consider and compare with your graphic novel collection.

Internet Movie Database (www.imdb.com). Search both "TV Episodes" and "Titles" to find plot synopses, character descriptions, and authors, all of which can be used when looking for graphic novel parallels and analogs.

A working knowledge of currently popular network television can also provide you with a boost when you are trying to figure out what tickles the fancy of a potential graphic novel reader who is a confirmed television viewer. Librarians who work with teens know the importance of being aware of popular culture; librarians who work with other age groups can find that such awareness sharpens their abilities to discuss what is important to this reader or potential reader.

Some examples of shared appeal factors for specific shows and books are shown in table 5.2.

Table 5.2
Moving from Television to Graphic Novel

SHARED APPEAL FACTORS	TV SHOW	GRAPHIC NOVEL
• Comedy romance • Adult female protagonist • Politically bland • Witty	*Gilmore Girls* (originally broadcast 2000–2007), with Lauren Graham and Alexis Bledel	Lucy Knisley's *French Milk* [a]
• Adventure/suspense • Male friends • Exaggerated sense of reality • Repertory approach to characters featured as central • Robust dialogue	*I Spy* (originally broadcast 1965–1968), with Bill Cosby and Robert Culp	Alan Moore and Dave Gibbons's *Watchmen* [b]
• Literary adaptation • PBS-level attention to writing, acting	*Jane Eyre* (Masterpiece Theatre version, 2006)	Posy Simmonds's *Gemma Bovery* [c]

[a] Lucy Knisley, *French Milk* (Touchstone, 2008).
[b] Alan Moore and Dave Gibbons, *Watchmen* (DC Comics, 1987).
[c] Posy Simmonds, *Gemma Bovery* (Pantheon, 2005).

AND GAMERS WITH A NARRATIVE BENT

The world of gaming is exploding and currently incorporates online, board, role-playing, and video options. Some games have distinct narrative elements to their unfolding, while others address the itch to practice a specific skill and best another player in that skill production. Role-playing has the most obvious story analog, but even some board games suggest an underlying narrative flow.

Game makers already publish some graphic novel correlatives that support and enhance the gaming side of their businesses. These are analogous, in terms of ease in identifying, to graphic novels that incorporate the characters and plotlines of screen arts. (An example of the latter is the series of Star Wars comics that interpret and expand storylines from the Star Wars movies.)[3] While game players of World of Warcraft may be happy to know about graphic novel versions of the game, this sort of recommendation requires little on the part of a readers' advisor; other gamers are more likely to inform the would-be comics reader of these books' existence than is the librarian, unless the staff member is quite familiar with the gaming universe.[4] Unlike *Star Wars* on paper, World of Warcraft in book format is dependent on the reader's knowledge of the specifics of the nonprint version of the narrative.

Plenty of games, however, do suggest graphic novel options for their fans. In order to operate as a readers' advisor in this corner of the narrative universe, you need to be familiar with the basic tenets of a variety of currently popular games, as well as aware of their players' general demographic breakdowns. For instance, role-playing games typically appeal more to people in their late teens through young adulthood than to seniors or children, more often to male than female participants. On the other hand, some board games such as Clue or Monopoly have long-standing and broad appeal across generations.[5] Electronic and online games vary widely in target participant appeal. Like movies and magazines, the gaming industry that relies on participant connectivity produces material suitable for various niche audiences.

Preparing yourself to provide advisory help to gamers seeking graphic novels, or seeking reading options that may include graphic novels, must include organizing your awareness of how different game formats work, which specific games are most likely to be known and played by your community's members, and correlative narrative features of those games.

Game Narrative

Do games have a narrative strand, or spine? Many do and many don't. While a game of bridge, like a game of tennis, follows a pattern, the movements in a game don't really tell a story. Clue, on the other hand, is an obvious narrative game, the entire point being to detect the narrative line. Between these two extremes lie a wide range of subtly shaded variations along the narrative scale. Some games force the players to create a narrative (as do role-playing ones) while others produce random plots (as does Clue).

What does this have to do with readers' advisory work with graphic novels? By discovering the gamer's taste in her games, the advisor can move to the most relevant offerings in the comics collection. Here are some trenchant questions to consider, although the excellent advisor will derive the information more subtly than by providing the would-be graphic novel reader with a checklist.

- What format game is of interest to the gamer: electronic, board, card-based, etc.?

- What is the shared theme of her favorite games? action, fantasy, tactical skill, etc.?
- How strong is the narrative element in these games?
- Are visual aspects of the games important or valued by this gamer?
- Which of the games she plays treat specific subjects, such as commerce, social classes, warfare, etc.?

Game Tools

The literature concerning gaming and libraries is growing exponentially. In addition to referring to professional material treating the possibilities for gamers in the library, the graphic novel readers' advisor should explore the world of gaming sufficiently to have a current working knowledge of popular, narrative-oriented games in every format. This doesn't mean you have to learn to play the games (although you might), but that you can involve a gamer in an appraisal of a game to derive ideas about taste and motivation that can be translated from games to graphic novels. Consider these resources:

Board Game Central (www.boardgamecentral.com) is a portal to descriptions of board and parlor games, sorted into genres and by likely participants.

Game Zone (www.gamezone.com) provides reviews of electronic games that are available both online and as software.

Gamertell (www.gamertell.com) provides electronic game reviews and image galleries and provides a sort by genre option.

THE NEXT KILLER APP

Readers' advisors can adapt the paradigm of "thinking global and acting local" to staying in touch with what's happening in other media. Today's readers are likely to exhibit increased media agnosticism, and the advisor can work with this cross-format interest in narrative and visual tastes to refine suggestions of graphic novels to suit interests suggested by the customer's concomitant tastes in visual and interactive media.

WHAT'S NEXT ...

In the next two chapters, you'll find graphic novel annotations that suggest the many doors and windows of topical and aesthetic entry points you have with which to assist readers.

Notes

1. Working with teachers at all levels to develop a better understanding of the fact that subscription databases, evaluated websites, audiobooks, podcasts, and visual arts can and do provide data as germane as that found in bound books has felt like a lifetime occupation to some youth-serving library staff.
2. Daniel Clowes, *Ghost World* (Seattle: Fantagraphics, 2001); and Clowes, *Eightball* (Seattle: Fantagraphics, 2004).
3. See the connections among movies, games, and books arising from the Star Wars concept at http://starwars.ugo.com/comics/default.asp.
4. World of Warcraft's home on the Web is www.worldofwarcraft.com/index.xml.
5. Clue and Monopoly, both published by Parker Brothers, are among several classic board games available in a number of editions that reflect local interests or players' skill levels.

6
BOOKS TO KNOW, PART A
Genres and Topics

Both traditional casual reading aids and the comprehensive graphic novel bibliographies described in chapter 8 tend to organize suggestions into alphabetical, topical, or genre lists. While alphabetical order provides a value-free ranking, ordering by genre or topic is a better step for many (but certainly not all) dedicated readers. Even this level of orientation to a collection of possibilities may be helpful to only a few who don't bring an initial interest to the list. However, as a tool for the advisor to use as he mediates a collection for a specific reader, or potential reader, a genre or topic list can be useful indeed.

DOS AND DON'TS FOR USING THESE LISTS

Readers' advisory work, at its best, is targeted to individuals or affinity groups. Genre and topical lists are necessarily organized around two or three points of commonality and thus carry content that differs in many ways. Those differences may be the subtle ones that make or break a choice for the reader who needs your advice. Don't assume that the titles listed are going to be equal in the eyes of your reader. Don't duck the invitation to work as a readers' advisor by offering a list instead of finding out what this reader wants, at this time, and bringing your knowledge of your collection along with your understanding of how lists are constructed to bear on your responses to this particular reader.

Do consider your community of advice seekers: Are they of a particular age or other demographic or affinity group? Are they experienced graphic novel readers or novices, or do they present a range of familiarity with the format?

DECODING THE LISTS

Individual titles are coded to suggest which ones are suitable to younger readers and which are friendly crossover choices for readers new to sequential art. Prolific graphic novel creators are also denoted, as are works translated from other languages. These are not comprehensive lists, but suggestions to jump-start your own analysis of the collection from which you are advising readers.

The following codes appear at the head of relevant entries, and are used to denote suggested audiences:

❋ appropriate for younger readers (under sixteen in some communities, as young as under twelve in others)

↔ crossover title for readers unfamiliar with the format

The following codes appear at the end of the annotation for relevant titles, and denote publishing contexts:

ⓔ instance of work by creator(s) with an extensive body of published sequential art including other graphic novels, comics, cartoons, or a combination of these formats

ⓣ English language edition is a translation

CONTEMPORARY REALISM

Abel, Jessica. *La Perdida* (Pantheon, 2006). A journey of self-exploration to Mexico by a young Latina from the United States is presented with credible bumps and fissures between expectations, wishes, and reality. Character development and expressive styles are provided visually in a complex narrative that relies on Spanish text as well as English.

Bell, Gabrielle. *Lucky* (Drawn and Quarterly, 2006). In this roman à clef, young artistic urbanites search for new accommodations and a dignified way of earning enough to maintain themselves and their art. Reportorial black-and-white images provide deep detail of both settings and nonverbal communications, while economically employed text carries the momentum of these episodes forward.

↔ Clowes, Daniel. *Ghost World* (Fantagraphics, 2001). Best friends spend the summer between high school and college—where they plan to continue pursuing their interest in visual art—engaged in worrying about the future and mercilessly teasing those who put up with them in the present. The full-color art is realistic enough that Clowes's film, which uses live action, resembles this drawn version of the people, the place, and the expressions of late adolescent angst. (E)

Cosey. *In Search of Shirley* (NBM, 1993). In two slim volumes, the story of Vietnam vets looking for the titular girl they once knew is filled with gorgeous landscapes in Italy and Vietnam, as well as generational questions such as discovering others' changes in shared middle age, the fate of Vietnam War orphans, and what might lie along the road less traveled. Realism and symbolism converge just as the text and images here work together to form the whole of the story. (E) (T)

✻ ↔ Fialkov, Joshua Hale, Noel Tuazon, and Scott A. Keating. *Elk's Run* (Villard, 2007). Adolescent rebellion comes to an isolationist enclave of armed social rebels in a ripped-from-possible-headlines intergenerational war story. Varying art styles convey essential aspects of time and psychological state without ever sacrificing character individuation or realistic expressiveness.

Lemire, Jeff. *Essex County* (Top Shelf Productions, 2007–2008, 2009). Available in three volumes or a Complete Essex County edition collecting *Tales from the Farm, Ghost Stories,* and *The Country Nurse,* the shared setting is rural Ontario. Lemire explores the lives of a handful of residents, including a bereaved boy and his bachelor uncle, brothers, and the local care providers. The clear and large images carry the weight of the narrative, although text supplies the reader's ear with local argot. (E)

Modan, Rutu. *Exit Wounds* (Drawn and Quarterly, 2007). A young man in Israel searches for his estranged father at the behest of a young woman soldier who asserts that he may have been killed in a bombing. Water coloring of the thinly drawn images provides visual context for the various landscapes of modern Israel—urban and rural—and tight plotting keeps the reader in the same suspense as the protagonist. (T)

Novgorodov, Danica. *Slow Storm* (First Second, 2008). Inky washes are well suited to showing the world of a midwesterner caught up in her career as a firefighter, tornado weather, and the travails of an illegal immigrant upon whom she chances. The storytelling here relies largely on images and the motion supplied by the reader's own interpretations of what happens between panels.

✻ Nowak, Naomi. *House of Clay* (NBM, ComicsLit, 2007). With color and line that offer a slightly pre-Raphaelite look to the art, the story of a young Frenchwoman who meets a number of strange and compelling characters when she finds work in a seaside sweatshop seems realistic until seemingly magical events begin to transpire. Symbolism in visual and plot elements abound.

Powell, Nate. *Swallow Me Whole* (Top Shelf Productions, 2008). Schizophrenia's effects on the youngest members of the patient's family are shown in deeply shadowed cartoon drawings in a plot that explores each family member's psychological weaknesses and doubts. Realistic close-ups and hallucinations share equal space with more traditional perspective.

↔ Rabagliati, Michel. *Paul Has a Summer Job* (Drawn and Quarterly, 2002). One of several realistic novels about artistic Paul, this outing recounts his first true experience with both earning a living and being responsible for the welfare of others. Leading city children through a wilderness camping experience is depicted with all its passing discomforts, gorgeous vistas, and interpersonal dramas for both kids and counselors. The visual style is both casually sketchy and finely detailed. Ⓔ Ⓣ

↔ Simmonds, Posy. *Tamara Drewe* (Houghton Mifflin, 2008). In this contemporary retelling of Thomas Hardy's *Far from the Madding Crowd,* the country estate of the sophisticated femme fatale neighbors on a writers' retreat and the local village population includes credibly bratty and star-obsessed schoolgirls. Imagery here is clear and nicely shaded, with characters' physicality connoting some of their personality traits and weaknesses. Ⓔ

Tomine, Adrian. *Shortcomings* (Drawn and Quarterly, 2007). Racial politics plays a role in the falling-out-of-love relationship between two young Asian Americans. Their cross-cultural urban world is depicted with realism both in image and plotting, but the realism is made accessible through skillful storytelling that invites the reader-viewer to share the characters' frustrations and doubts rather than judge them from the outside. Ⓔ

↔ Wood, Brian, and Ryan Kelly. *Local* (Oni Press, 2008). A young woman explores her possibilities for identity by visiting a dozen cities in North America. The finely detailed black-and-white images portray each city authentically while also depicting the changes evoked in her. At first, these read like related but unconnected stories, but just past the halfway point, it becomes clear that there is a plot element that is progressing and moving the series toward a unifying conclusion. Ⓔ

MYSTERY AND DETECTION

Baker, Kyle. *You Are Here* (DC Comics, Vertigo, 1998). In full color, a small-time criminal who wants to impress his new girlfriend instead winds up fighting for his life at the hands of a murderer. High-octane action fuels this not-very-serious genre entry, in which text is as rich as the artwork. Ⓔ

Clowes, Daniel. *Ice Haven* (Pantheon, 2005). A range of artwork correlated to the various characters' personalities and viewpoints express the reactions of a small town to the disappearance of one of their children. Satire is more important here than whodunit. Ⓔ

❇ Geary, Rick. *The Lindbergh Child* (NBM, 2009). Following on the project of documenting Victorian murders of note (Treasury of Victorian Murder), this series opener featuring twentieth-century cases (Treasury of XXth Century Murder) explores the perception of heroism and villainy as part of the factual account of the unsolved Charles Lindbergh infant kidnap-murder case. Images here provide perspective as well as details revealing connections between people and evidence. Ⓔ

↔ Hubert and Kerascoet. *Miss Don't Touch Me* (NBM, 2008). When her sister is murdered and the serial assailant eludes police, a young woman in post–Great War Paris does some skillful—and accidental—sleuthing on her own. Lush watercolors depict the excitement of the streetscapes, the frightening nighttime shadows and the details of the upscale brothel where the young woman sets up detective shop. Ⓣ

❇ Johnson, Mat, and Warren Pleece. *Incognegro* (DC Comics, Vertigo, 2008). Chiaroscuro art provides the right look and feel for a story that takes its model from a real murder case that unfolded ninety years ago. It's not the murder that's center stage here, but the racial tensions of the time and place (Mississippi) and the lynch mob mentality that replaced anything like a just inquiry.

❇ Lapham, David, and Dan Lapham. *Silverfish* (DC Comics, Vertigo, 2007). Whether it's adolescent distrust of parents and their chosen partners or a real murder hovering in the shadows is the question explored from a couple of viewpoints. Scary, inky black-and-white images capture the mundane as well as the atmospheric, the concrete realities of babysitting an asthmatic little sister, and the mystery of psychotic hallucinations, in a genre-bending bit of noir.

Legrand and Jacque Tardi. *Roach Killer* (NBM, 1992). By turns mysterious, complicated, and violent, this tale of an exterminator who has the misfortune to overhear a murder plot unfolds in a highly detailed rendering of Manhattan. Narrative and art in this story are not evenly matched, so this is more rewarding for visually inclined readers than for those wanting a literary plot. Ⓔ Ⓣ

↔ Rucka, Greg, and Steve Lieber. *Whiteout* (Oni Press, 2007). Antarctica proves a fantastic setting for a serial killer story and the female U.S. Marshal who won't give up until she identifies the killer and then gets her man. Black-and-white sketchwork makes the climate look as cold, barren, and weather-bombarded as it is, here and in the sequel *Melt* (Oni Press, 2007). Ⓔ

HISTORICAL FICTION

❊ Abouet, Marguerite, and Clément Oubrerie. *Aya* (Drawn and Quarterly, 2007). Ivory Coast in the late 1970s supported a middle class that relied on American corporations and allowed girls to advance their educations. Aya is one such girl, although her midlevel manufacturing manager father doesn't think she should continue on to college and her girlfriends are getting themselves into traditional trouble with boys. Beautifully watercolored and highly expressive cartoon art offers an intimate look into Aya's world, where she is more observer— and a smart one at that—than actor. This opens a series that continues with *Aya of Yop City* (Drawn and Quarterly, 2008) and will hold other sequels as well. Ⓣ

Katchor, Ben. *The Jew of New York* (Pantheon, 2000). Set during the middle of the nineteenth century, this fantastic tale features sardonic political commentary, anti-Semitic burlesque, and popular science of the period. Scratchboard-like drawing is washed over to offer soft grays that further blur the lines between real events and imaginative what-might-have-happeneds. Ⓔ

❊ Klein, Grady. *The Lost Colony* (First Second, 2006–). Each story in this symbol-laden but accessible satire exposes some of the largest myths and misdeeds that have created popular understanding of American history and characters. Candy-colored cartoons and a cast of folkloric characters carry forward through *The Snodgrass Conspiracy, The Red Menace,* and *Last Rights,* each of which is set in an alternative antebellum paradise for white men—and at the heart of which is a little girl whose best friends aren't white.

Nakazawa, Keiji. *Barefoot Gen* (Last Gasp, 2004–2009). The English translation of the author's fictionalized account of his boyhood experiences as a victim of Hiroshima's atom bombing, this title has reached eight volumes. Written thirty years ago as manga for his own countrymen, the author's use of cultural tropes and themes, both visual and characterizing, are universally accessible. Ⓔ Ⓣ

Sfar, Joann. *Klezmer* (First Second, 2006). In the first of proposed multiple volumes, the picaresque ancestry of Eastern Jewish folk music serves as the catalyst for a tale of wandering, murder, and jokes lobbed as defensive weapons. The squiggly lined artwork is washed with watercolor that gives nearly every panel a distinct but sometimes monochrome identity. See also its companion *The Rabbi's Cat* (Pantheon, 2005). Ⓔ Ⓣ

Stassen, J. P. *Deogratias: A Tale of Rwanda* (First Second, 2006). The Rwandan Genocide was rooted in the country's Belgian colonial past. In vivid painterly color, and with complexity of narrative that addresses the confluent effects of colonialism, the Church, and intertribal traditions, the story shows how the individual becomes a violent person he would not be and is driven to the edge of insanity by it. Ⓣ

❋ ↔ Sturm, James. *James Sturm's America: God, Gold, and Golems* (Drawn and Quarterly, 2007). Here are collected three novellas based on American history: *The Revival, Hundreds of Feet Below Daylight,* and perhaps Sturm's most familiar baseball story, *The Golem's Mighty Swing.* Different drawing styles convey the three time periods, with the nineteenth-century religious revival and the mining story in rough black and white, and the Negro Leagues–era tale in sepia-washed and softer shapes. Ⓔ

Trondheim, Lewis, and Olivier Appollodorus. *Bourbon Island 1730* (First Second, 2008). As truth-grounded and adventurous as Stevenson's *Treasure Island,* this pirate story is set on Réunion Island at a time when pirates and former slaves unite against colonization. Trondheim's hallmark use of animal faces to characterize individuals and beautiful watercoloring make this visually pleasing and complex while the narrative's high adventure is consistently authentic emotionally as well as historically. Ⓔ Ⓣ

Vance, James, and Dan Burr. *Kings in Disguise* (Kitchen Sink, 1990). This iconic road story set during the Great Depression is realistic in plot and black-and-white depictions of boxcar journeys, break-ins, and protest marches. This shows the American landscape accurately while conveying details of the fictional characters as though they were real.

✳ ↔ Vaughan, Brian K., and Niko Henrichon. *Pride of Baghdad* (DC Comics, Vertigo, 2006). Inspired by a true event, when lions escaped from the Baghdad Zoo after it was hit by a bomb in 2003, this beautifully colored story tells what happens from the lions' viewpoints. Other episodes in human history that have touched wildlife are woven into the lions' story. (E)

FANTASY AND SCIENCE FICTION

✳ Abel, Jessica, Gabriel Soria, and Warren Pleece. *Life Sucks* (First Second, 2008). Goth girl meets vegetarian vampire in this finely orchestrated story of difficult attractions. The multiethnic cast is drawn looking contemporary Los Angeles slacker-enervated but in full color. (E)

Burns, Charles. *Black Hole* (Pantheon, 2005). Deformity is one of the horrible side effects of a sexually transmitted disease plaguing Seattle. Symbolism, surrealism, and a frightening degree of realism are mixed seamlessly in the black-and-white drawings and the narrative itself. (E)

Carey, Mike, and John Bolton. *God Save the Queen* (DC Comics, Vertigo, 2007). Faeries and heroin make a bloody mix in this well-constructed story. Set in London and featuring contemporary teens and rough squats that are atmospherically rendered in color and framing that heighten the suspense, this riff on Shakespeare works visually and as a tightly worked narrative. (E)

✳ Carré, Lilli. *The Lagoon* (Fantagraphics, 2008). Some benevolent spirit, as well as the more natural wildlife, keeps harmony with a multigenerational family living near its lagoon. In addition to loopy black-and-white art, the narrative is moved along by an accompanying soundtrack of natural and musical emanations from both the people and the creatures in this symbol-rich and gentle story.

Chadwick, Paul. *Concrete* (Dark Horse, 2005–). Short stories featuring an eco-active, intelligent, and socially engaged fellow who is trapped in the rocklike body of a monster are being republished in volumes that trace his origins and continuing saga. Additional stories in each black-and-white volume featuring this character include some horror but typically more introspective and sometimes autobiographical pieces. Perspective and human expressiveness, along with engaging text and plotting, reveal continual surprises. (E)

Cosby, Andrew, Michael Alan Nelson, and Greg Scott. *X Isle* (Boom! Studios, 2007). Evolution has taken a different and frightening course on the island where a scientific team explores. Deep shadows and lots of visual detail in a range of situations from the known and mundane world of tourists and shipboard life to close-up views of imagined species heighten the full-color realism and moodiness of the art. (E)

❋ ↔ De Crecy, Nicolas. *Glacial Period* (NBM, ComicsLit, 2007). In the far distant future, archaeologists cut through ice to discover and be mystified by the Louvre and its vast collections. Fully colored and cleverly visually detailed, this is the first in a series commissioned by the Louvre to help show its work to readers. See also Marc-Antoine Mathieu's *Museum Vaults: Excerpts from the Journal of an Expert* (NBM, ComicsLit, 2008) for another take on the project, also utilizing a science fiction approach. (E) (T)

Dezago, Todd, Craig Rousseau, and Rico Renzi. *The Perhapanauts* (Dark Horse, 2006). Traditional mythic fellows, including Sasquatch, become the guardians of the known world when it's invaded by really bad unbeings. Clear lines and bright colors underscore the not-too-serious nature of this cosmic opera.

❋ ↔ Kim, Derek Kirk, and Jesse Hamm. *Good as Lily* (Minx, 2007). When dead Lily's little sister Grace turns eighteen and is accidentally hit on the head on her birthday, she is confronted by herself at four different ages, past and future. Realistically hip black-and-white American manga art shows off the mostly Asian American cast in a series of poignant and funny efforts to just get along. (E)

❋ Kochalka, James. *Monkey vs. Robot and the Crystal of Power* (Top Shelf Productions, 2003). Naïf flat drawings, lacking shading but offering surprising amounts of expression, tell most of the story in this nature versus technology riff. (E)

❋ McCloud, Scott. *The New Adventures of Abraham Lincoln* (Image Comics, 1998). Brightly colored cartoon art, with script that's computer-generated rather than the traditional hand-drawn, this story features a very young hero who discovers how outer space aliens intend to take over the United States through the clever employment of patriotic lapel pins. Satire and pop cultural references add humor to the adventure. (E)

✳ Mills, Scott. *The Masterplan* (Top Shelf Productions, 2003). The expansion of the universe is perceived by one scientist as a threat, and he sets out to stop it. Deceptively simple and soft black-and-white drawing, held tightly in small, square panels with the occasional full-page spread, show as well as tell the scientist's concern for containment of the possible. Ⓔ

Nantsuki, Kioichi, and Yuki Miyoshi. *Samurai Shodown* (Viz, 1997). In eighteenth-century Japan, three traditional warriors must take on forces that are inhuman, battling to protect their land and all Earth from a supernatural enemy. The sound of swordplay and look of warrior strength are depicted with a manga sense for outsized emphasis. Ⓣ

Pope, Paul. *Heavy Liquid* (DC Comics, Vertigo, 2001). In a near-future city brought to life in color washes and the depiction of credibly updated transports, a substance that is both a banned recreational drug and material for construction creates the set-up for a high-tech thriller. The creation of futuristic cityscapes and scary encounters are compellingly achieved through impressionistic washes of black ink highlighted with luridly bright pigments. Ⓔ

Sfar, Joann. *The Rabbi's Cat* (Pantheon, 2005). Set in the Algerian Jewish community before World War II, this archly told compilation of family stories and traditional inquiries is narrated by a talking cat. Brightly colored with expressive and idiosyncratic creatures—animal and human—this combines humanism, theology, and fantasy. A second volume (2008) continues the story with a cat-led quest for the African Jerusalem. Ⓔ Ⓣ

✳ Sfar, Joann, and Emmanuel Guibert. *The Professor's Daughter* (First Second, 2007). Victorian London was crazy for Egyptian artifacts, but that can't have prepared one academic and middle-class father for his daughter's love for and marriage to an ancient Egyptian mummified pharaoh. Told with tongue firmly in cheek, the graceful and pastel painted art enhances both the details of the setting and the humorous take on events. Ⓔ Ⓣ

✳ Yang, Gene Luen, and Derek Kirk Kim. *The Eternal Smile and Other Stories* (First Second, 2009). Three stories rendered in three visual styles each rely on a hairpin turn in the plot. Fully colored and riffing on traditional "days of yore" fantasy, funny animal stories, and the foibles of modern e-mail-based swindling, each tale relies on visual as well as verbal content to fully yield its satire as well as poignancy. Ⓔ

ROMANCE

Hernandez, Gilbert. *Palomar: The Heartbreak Soup Stories* (Fantagraphics, 2003). The Hernandez brothers have been creating and recreating a soap opera universe (Love and Rockets) for decades. This collection from it features the magic realism of characters Chelo and Luba as they lead hectic lives in a Latin American location. Black-and-white art provides full characterization in narratives that turn to midwifery, tourists, and difficult men. Ⓔ

Hernandez, Jaime. *The Education of Hopey Glass* (Fantagraphics, 2008). This collection of short stories gives entrée into the Locas universe peopled by Latina girlfriends, a bit of murder, and lots of attempts at finding true love. The black ink art utilizes saturated patterns for shading and offers deeply expressive faces and postures. Ⓔ

Kneece, Mark, and Julie Collins-Rousseau. *Trailers* (NBM, ComicsLit, 2005). A trailer park youth works hard to protect his younger siblings from their evil and violent mother, even going so far as to help her hide the body of the man she's murdered. His involvement with a beautiful and normal girl at school contrasts and heightens the terror with which he lives at home. Realistically detailed images of the seamy and more hopeful aspects of his life add flesh to the plot's bones. Ⓔ

✳ Kwitney, Aisa, and Joelle Jones. *Token* (Minx, 2008). A teenage girl reacts to her father's new relationship by creating one of her own, choosing a mysterious Latino boy who teaches her how to shoplift and, eventually, how to kiss. Beautifully rendered characters and Florida settings provide depth and texture to a tale that portrays the difficulties of becoming an individual instead of part of a relationship.

Lutes, Jason. *Jar of Fools* (Drawn and Quarterly, 2003). Magic isn't necessarily a cure for romantic or practical problems, but it lends flexibility to how the characters here can interact. Flat black-and-white cartoons present silent passages between those that carry text as the repertory cast explores aging, loss, and wistful hope in a prosaic coffee shop and on the magician's stage.

Marvit, Lawrence. *Sparks: An Urban Fairytale* (Slave Labor Graphics, 2002). A young woman mechanic from an unstable home builds herself the perfect boyfriend—from engine parts. Retro-tinged black ink art shows a different reality from the one of the narrator's imaginative spin on her sometimes scary real life.

Moore, Terry. *Strangers in Paradise: High School* (Abstract Studio, 1999). Part of the lengthy and developmentally ordered Strangers in Paradise series, this episode details how the relationship between the main characters began. Detailed drawings with almost no shading show mundane and scene-setting detail as well as incisive facial and postural expressions.

Sfar, Joann. *Vampire Loves* (First Second, 2006). An elegant vampire who has just broken off with a young woman looks high and low for a satisfying replacement partner. His friends include a talking tree and a witch, with a golem and a cat also playing significant roles in these adventures. Beautifully watercolored cartoon art evokes both a sense of reality and stately silliness. The vampire is the adult version of the one featured in Sfar's children's stories, *Little Vampire* (First Second, 2008). Ⓔ Ⓣ

✳ Thompson, Craig. *Good-bye, Chunky Rice* (Pantheon, 2006). A sweet and insightful tale of friendship, the competing need for independence, and the desire to share new discoveries with an old friend is told through the agency of a mouse, a turtle, and assorted human misfits. Thompson's cartoons are set in panels that pop the action out from the page and make even the potentially shocking instead awe- and empathy-inspiring.

Wood, Brian, and Ryan Kelly. *The New York Four* (Minx, 2008). Set in a realistic New York University neighborhood, this story shows contemporary young adult life that comes with communicating in pithy text messages, searching for balance between study and desire, and the struggle to demonstrate independence to both family and peers. Photorealistic art as well as more traditionally comic book sketches support this realistic storyline. Ⓔ

SUSPENSE AND HORROR

Christin, Pierre, and Enki Bilal. *The Black Order Brigade* (Humanoids, 2002). In this political thriller, Fascist militants from the Spanish Civil War again roam village streets, murdering for the sake of old grudges. International efforts to confront the menace move the scene among several modern European cities and what would be bucolic countryside except for the deadly menace. Brilliantly watercolored artwork shows realistic details from wrinkled faces to gunshot wounds. Ⓔ Ⓣ

Golden, Christopher, Tom Sniegoski, and Paul Azaceta. *Talent* (Boom! Studios, 2007). The young adult horror writer turns to graphic novel suspense in the form of a plane crash survivor who is being chased because he now channels the dead. Color washes over stylized comics add emotional tones ranging from ominous to revelatory.

❋ Madison, Ivory, and Cliff Richards. *Huntress: Year One* (DC Comics, 2009). In this version of the superhero mythology, Batman's universe is overshadowed by a tale of the Sicilian Mafia. Fully realized characters in a brilliantly colored environment that includes church interiors, middle-class and Cosa Nostra homes, and, of course, urban rooftops play out a moral tale filled with tension that has political and religious, as well as crime-fighting, roots. **(E)**

Moore, Alan, and Oscar Zarate. *A Small Killing* (Avatar Press, 2003). *Watchmen* author Moore here tells the story of an Everyman stalked by a demonic and murderous child. Full-color paintings show realistic foregrounds in haunting backdrops. **(E)**

Rapp, Adam, and George O'Connor. *Ball Peen Hammer* (First Second, 2009). This bloody dystopian tale centers on a man with the job of dispensing with the bodies of murdered children. The full-color images are harrowing but carry the narrative forward as the protagonist longs for the woman who, unbeknownst to him, hides in another part of his apartment building, and works to overcome his moral qualms at carrying out his allotted job.

Wilson, G. Willow, and M. K. Perker. *Cairo* (DC Comics, Vertigo, 2007). This genre-blending novel is firmly set in the modern Egyptian city and shows how the place can be both sanctuary and threat to the tourist, drug dealer, Israeli soldier, guerilla, and reporter who are brought together by a plot that stretches from magic realism to political thriller. The visual element here is stronger than the narrative flow, showing off aspects of the city that are, by turns, mysterious and cosmopolitan. **(E)**

BIOGRAPHY AND MEMOIR

B., David. *Epileptic* (Pantheon, 2005). From the vantage point of a younger sibling, David B. recalls his family's quest to find relief for the grand mal seizures experienced by his brother from late childhood. Unshaded saturated black ink shows middle-class French life in the last quarter of the twentieth century as a series of diet regimes, trips to gurus and special camps, and the lasting effects of these efforts on the younger children. Ⓔ Ⓣ

Bechdel, Alison. *Fun Home: A Family Tragicomic* (Houghton Mifflin, 2004). Coming out gay is something the author achieved in spite of her father's inability to do the same. This memoir, which turned to her childhood journals as a source, speaks eloquently to the psychological and social battles fought and left unfought in this fraught family dynamic. Cross-hatched shading and occasional color washes lend depth to the art. Ⓔ

Brown, Chester. *Louis Riel* (Drawn and Quarterly, 2004). The life of the nineteenth-century Canadian French–Native American leader is presented with documentary care and aesthetically fitting austerity. Small, uniform panels, elegantly shaded and with unusual angles, show Riel's life with its concomitant charismatic power, threat of insanity, and eventual capital punishment. Ⓔ

↔ Carey, Percy, and Ronald Wimberly. *Sentences: The Life of M. F. Grimm* (DC Comics, Vertigo, 2007). After a childhood performing in *Sesame Street* and young adulthood as a hip-hop star, the author was sentenced to prison on drug charges—and to life in a wheelchair as a paraplegic. Pencil shading gives the realistic and rough-edged artwork a hip-hop look that suits the memoir.

Fleming, Ann Marie. *The Magical Life of Long Tack Sam* (Riverhead Books, 2007). Fleming explores the life and career of her Chinese great-grandfather, a magician and performer who traveled the world and made her family a fully multiethnic one. Black ink washes are highlighted with occasional color, and the use of photographs, bits of documents, and other realia add to the visual texture of the narrative.

Geary, Rick. *J. Edgar Hoover* (Hill and Wang, 2008). Neither a sanitized nor tabloid version of the controversial FBI founder's life, this biography shows how human, fallible, and contradictory the man was in both his political and private affairs. Geary's hallmark reportorial black-and-white drawings utilize differentiations in panel size, shape, and placement, helping to convey influences that made the man and how the man influenced events in the criminal justice and political spheres of the twentieth century. Ⓔ

↔ Guibert, Emmanuel. *Alan's War: The Memories of G. I. Alan Cope* (First Second, 2008). After World War II, Cope resettled in France, where, late in his life, he met Guibert and told him of his wartime experiences. Guided by Cope's memories and adjustments to his early drafts, Guibert retells the story of a young American sent to Europe to fight and where he learned about politics, love, and affection for the countryside. Small, softly shaded panels show realistic details and image and text are tightly bound to create the narrative. Ⓔ Ⓣ

Ka, Alfred, and Olivier Ka. *Why I Killed Peter* (NBM, 2008). Sexual abuse at the hands of a priest is treated here with sensitivity and intelligence by the victim. Showing how the priest gained his and his family's trust for years before assaulting him in his early adolescence, and how the victim spent more years before confronting his assailant, the scratchy color cartoons eventually give way, as the story progresses, to the realism of camera snapshots. Ⓣ

✳ ↔ Obomsawin, Diane. *Kaspar* (Drawn and Quarterly, 2009). The story of Kaspar Hauser, the mysterious early nineteenth-century youth who appeared as a foundling without memory of human society, is told from Hauser's viewpoint, in simple drawings and with his own words as the source for the narrative. Ⓣ

↔ Pekar, Harvey, and others. *The Beats: A Graphic History* (Hill and Wang, 2009). This collective biography and critical literary analysis of the works and lives of Jack Kerouac, Lawrence Ferlinghetti, Diane di Prima, and others in the Beat circle unfolds in a series of pen-and-ink sequential art essays by a variety of contemporary cartoonists and writers, including Lance Tooks, Peter Kuper, and Ed Piskor. The art is informed by both the Beat ethos and the passage of time since it was the mark of the modern. Ⓔ

Satrapi, Marjane. *The Complete Persepolis* (Pantheon, 2007). From the Islamic Revolution of her childhood through her teen experiences in a Swiss boarding school and young womanhood in Tehran and abroad, this explores both one woman's formative years and the changes in her politically charged culture. Heavily inked cartoons show her apprenticeship to David B. while carrying her unique narrative. Ⓣ

Schrag, Ariel. *Potential* (Simon and Schuster, 2008). As a high school student, the author came to celebratory terms with her sexual orientation, while also coping with her parents' rocky marriage and her friends' shaky psychological states. All the while, she recorded these experiences as her own sequential art autobiography, in which she appears as a small, big-eyed tomboy in an authentically depicted Berkeley. See the prequels and sequel, completing her high school career, in *Awkward and Definition* (Simon and Schuster, 2008), which Schrag originally published herself as a teen, and *Likewise* (Simon and Schuster, 2009).

Thompson, Craig. *Blankets* (Top Shelf Productions, 2003). After a childhood fraught with the peril of strict and surly parents with rigorous religious views, Thompson discovered the potential of freedom at the same time that he found his first true love. All this is rendered in soft pencil, with human proportions that bespeak character and relationship rather than actual physical appearance.

POPULAR SCIENCE

❄ ↔ Gonick, Larry. *The Cartoon Guide to Physics* (HarperPerennial, 1991). Part of a series in which hard and applied sciences are explained through humor and image as much as through facts, this volume uses a cartoon hostess and a cast of funny-looking guys engaged in activities like race car driving to break down big concepts into accessible situations. Ⓔ

❄ ↔ Hosler, Jay. *Clan Apis* (Active Synapse, 2000). The social and biological life of the honeybee is presented through the life story of one. Clever plotting and clear depictions of bee anatomy, colonies, and ecosystems in large black-and-white drawings include lore related to bees and honey as well as scientific fact. See the scientist-author's *Sandwalk* (Active Synapse, 2003) as well for a story that informs about evolution.

↔ Ottaviani, Jim, and others. *Two-Fisted Science* (G. T. Labs, 2001). Nearly a dozen well-known comics artists worked with a scientist on this collection of essays describing the work of Galileo, Richard Feynman, Hans Bohr, and other men whose scientific inquiries have created our modern understanding of the universe. Artwork, all in black and white, varies from orderly ink drawings to shadowy pencil and impressionistic cartoons. See also the companion volume, featuring the work of women of science, *Dignifying Science* (G. T. Labs, 2003). Ⓔ

❄ Schultz, Mark, Zander Cannon, and Kevin Cannon. *The Stuff of Life* (Hill and Wang, 2009). Anthropomorphic cells, cartoons in period dress, and talking animals help relate the history of the science of genetics. The usually crowded and detailed panels offer solid information in black and white, while the narrative includes biographic and political details as well as verbal explanations of mechanics.

HISTORY AND POLITICS

Anderson, Ho Che. *King: A Comics Biography of Martin Luther King, Jr.* (Fantagraphics, 2005). Originally published in three volumes across a decade, this comprehensive study of King's life and the meaning of his work and reception in contemporary America is based on research and primary source interviews. A wide array of art styles, including silhouette, saturated color washes, photo montages, and sketches, is used to convey King's personality as well as events of the Civil Rights Era. **(E)**

Baker, Kyle. *Nat Turner* (Abrams, 2008). The story of the slave-led rebellion in Antebellum Virginia is recounted in full color and minimal use of text. This method of conveying the nuanced influence of Turner's strength and leadership relies on careful pacing. **(E)**

Blanchet, Paul. *White Rapids* (Drawn and Quarterly, 2007). The birth and eventual abandonment of a town built and maintained by a power company offers an evocative view on modern Western corporate power. Full-page, period-piece two-color art captures the evolution from forest through planned town to decay, with the people involved depicted in keeping with mid-twentieth-century "good versus evil" cartoon features. **(E) (T)**

Briggs, Raymond. *When the Wind Blows* (Schocken, 1982). The vagaries of Cold War Era "preparation" of Westerners to combat nuclear disaster are shown in this fable-like story. Tiny panels interspersed with full-page images tell the tale of a middle-aged working-class British couple who believe they can "hide" from the fallout, with bright coloring highlighting both the daily reality of their lives and the drama of the explosion. **(E)**

Eisner, Will. *A Life Force* (Norton, 2006). The Great Depression and the rise of Nazi power changed many lives around the world at a philosophical as well as practical level. One such life is depicted here in Eisner's iconic, detailed, black-and-white collection of three previously published books, *Life on Dropsie Avenue, A Contract with God,* and *A Life Force.* Ⓔ

Gantz, David. *Jews in America* (Jewish Lights Publishing, 2006). For five hundred years, Jews have been part of American history. Here, with wit and in black ink art, some of the scenes in which they have found themselves, and in others they created, tell the bones of that history. Ⓔ

✳ Jensen, Derrik, and Stephanie McMillan. *As the World Burns: 50 Simple Things You Can Do to Stay in Denial* (Seven Stories Press, 2007). Environmental policy and the popular "simple things you can do" prescription both receive satiric and insight-provoking treatment. Flat black-and-white art with no straight lines and featuring oddities such as a one-eyed rabbit, lead the narrative that pits an optimist against a realist in this eco-wasteland where correction isn't simple but demands action.

✳ ↔ Laird, Roland, and Elihu Bey. *Still I Rise* (Norton, 1998). Offering not just African American history but American history from the African American viewpoint, this simply illustrated narrative provides context and highlights issues that have been and are formed by race relations in the United States from its foundation.

✳ ↔ Llewelyn, Morgan, Michael Scott, and Eoin Coveney. *Ireland: A Graphic History* (Element, 1995). The wash of Ireland's political and cultural history is recounted in a series of tales bound together by the flight of a raven and lovers lost to each other in the throes of political upheaval. Large and deeply colored panels highlight the details of physical appearances and ways of living as those evolve through the centuries from Newgrange to modern Belfast.

Miller, Frank, and Lynn Varley. *300* (Dark Horse, 1999). Blood flows freely and in vivid color across the large pages in this retelling of the Battle of Thermopylae. Visual details present most of the information, with text providing only the words necessary to convey communication between characters. Dramatic intercuts of scenes and actions, as well as concentrated details, amplify the battle's roar. Ⓔ

Murphy, Justin, and Al Milgrom. *Cleburne* (Rampart Press, 2008). General Patrick Cleburne organized a Confederate unit composed of emancipated slaves during the American Civil War. Here, the perspective on events as seen by a woman and battle scenes presented in overlapping panels that lend realism to the depicted action are among the visual riches brought to retelling this chapter of history.

↔ Sacco, Joe. *Safe Area Gorazde: The War in Eastern Bosnia, 1992–1995* (Fantagraphics, 2000). Professional cartoon journalist Sacco explores the U.N. safe zone town through several informants as well as his own eyewitness. The mundane details of daily life where the electricity is gone but American jeans are held in high premium, as well as the fearful journeys into and out of the demilitarized area, are depicted in large black-and-white pages, with Sacco himself evident in many reports, showing the reporter's real relationship to the story. See also the prequel, *The Fixer* (Drawn and Quarterly, 2003) and the sequel, *War's End* (Drawn and Quarterly, 2005). Ⓔ

Satrapi, Marjane. *Embroideries* (Pantheon, 2006). The lives and life-affirming skills of Iranian women are depicted through their stories, with their images shown unbounded by panels or even much expression. The flat black-and-white pages are reminiscent of shadows seen through a curtain, just as the women's real lives are mostly led out of public view. Ⓔ Ⓣ

❋ Spiegelman, Art. *The Complete Maus* (Pantheon, 1996). Presenting the Holocaust and its continuing effects on survivors and their children through a cast that includes anthropomorphic Nazi cats, Jewish mice, Polish pigs, and so on, cartoonist and sequential art theorist Speigelman demonstrates the fully realized potential of graphic novel narrative semantics and imagery. Ⓔ

Zinn, Howard, Mike Konopacki, and Paul Buhle. *A People's History of American Empire* (Metropolitan Books, 2008). Using a different historical person to narrate each section in this collection of events that demonstrate U.S. imperialism, political historian Zinn and artist Konopacki combine talents for storytelling and characterization. In addition to drawing, there is selective and effective use made here of document copies and archival photographs.

TRAVEL

Delisle, Guy. *Pyongyang: A Journey in North Korea* (Drawn and Quarterly, 2005). In grays and blacks, the French animator who traveled to the usually closed society of contemporary North Korea offers a window on the residents' grim daily lives. Sardonic tourist suggestions are included, as are sympathetic views of how this warping of cultural identity has created vistas and sightseeing opportunities unknown in freer places. See also Delisle's *Shenzhen: A Travelogue from China* (Drawn and Quarterly, 2006) and *The Burma Chronicles* (Drawn and Quarterly, 2008) for more of his empathetic but acute observations on life in Asia. Ⓔ Ⓣ

Goff, Cindy, Rafael Nieves, and Seitu Hayden. *The Temporary Natives* (Epic Comics, 1990). Peace Corps workers in Central Africa confront the fact that their presence can't change either the political fate of the nation's people or themselves. See also the companion in the Tales from the Heart of Africa series, *Bloodlines* (Epic Comics, 1992).

Knisley, Lucy. *French Milk* (Simon and Schuster, 2008). Just before completing her undergraduate work in art, the American author traveled with her mother to Paris for a long vacation. This journal captures in pencil and snapshots her impressions of the city and its natives, personal concerns about her future, and discoveries in markets and at cafés.

London, Andrew. *Jeremy Pickle Goes to Prague* (Fantagraphics, 1996). London describes the Czech city from his experiences there as an admiring tourist and cartoonist. This non-Fodor's approach nonetheless offers informative bits as well as visual gags.

Martinson, Lars. *Tonoharu* (Top Shelf Productions, 2008–). Looking back at the author's experiences of trying to live comfortably in Japan while assisting in a middle school classroom, this roman à clef shows the difference between romantic expectations and the reality of living abroad. Dainty shading of the realistic images amplifies the mood and heightens the sense of Japanese decorum.

Rall, Ted. *To Afghanistan and Back* (NBM, 2003). A cartoon journalist who had previous experience traveling in Afghanistan portrays his three-week visit during the American bombing after September 11. His uninhibited and rough drawing style well matches his anti-jingoist and anti-idealist reporting voice. Ⓔ

❉ Steinberger, Aimee Major. *Japan Ai: A Tall Girl's Adventure in Japan* (Go! Comi, 2007). Anime fan Steinberger traveled to her beloved Japan with a couple of friends. Here she shows how they coped with Japanese toilets, clothing too small to fit her large frame, and traveling without a good grasp of the local language. Manga-style art suits this tourist report, of course, and is occasionally colored to highlight some milestone moments in the visit.

↔ Trondheim, Lewis. *Little Nothings: The Curse of the Umbrella* (NBM, ComicsLit, 2008). The famous French cartoonist publishes regular collections of his cartoon blog and in this volume there's a lot of traveling and travel worries. Trondheim travels for work—among the destinations is Angoulême—and for pleasure—to Latin America and the tropics—and his little, full-color panels provoke incisive observations on both the locals and tourists as a demographic. Ⓔ Ⓣ

RELIGION

Baker, Kyle. *King David* (DC Comics, Vertigo, 2002). The biblical heavy-hitter receives pop icon treatment in this humorous and colorful rendition of his many adventures. Broad humor is employed irreverently but the dominant themes of goodness and godliness aren't lost. Both computer art and free-hand drawing were used to create these images. Ⓔ

✳ ↔ Katin, Miriam. *We Are on Our Own* (Drawn and Quarterly, 2006). Precipitated by experiences in the Holocaust, the author's family struggles with issues of faith and how to raise children in a tradition without religious belief. Stark black-and-white images are offset with dramatic uses of red.

↔ Mack, Stan. *The Story of the Jews: A 4,000-Year Adventure* (Jewish Lights Publishing, 2001). Political, social, and religious history all get treated with humor, insight, and high energy in this accurate rendition of who the Jews have been and are, and how they got that way. Visually, this bouncy black-and-white cartoon history includes fine detail, explanatory charts, and true character. Ⓔ

✳ Page, Tyler. *Nothing Better* (Demention Comics, 2007). In the course of her freshman year at college, a young woman moves from unreflective acceptance of her inherited Lutheran identity to a fuller exploration of what faith is and what role it has in daily life. This bildungsroman shows authentic contemporary college life as well as character interactions that could have been word-heavy, but here are fully communicated with a balance of image and text.

✳ Saiwai, Tetsu. *The 14th Dalai Lama* (Emotional Content, 2008). Manga-style black-and-white comics shaded with a variety of patterns are used to tell the life story, to date, of the Tibetan religious and political leader. Crisp narrative and expressive faces and postures invest this account with high accessibility for those who may already be fans of the Dalai Lama as well as those who come to his story with little previous knowledge.

↔ Tezuka, Osamu. *Buddha* (Vertical, 2003–2005). In eight translated volumes, the father of Japanese comics provides a comprehensive study of the Buddha's life, philosophy, and influences on world cultures. Appropriate to manga, both comedic and dramatically violent episodes are depicted on a grand scale. Ⓔ Ⓣ

✱ Yang, Gene Luen. *Loyola Chin and the San Peligran Order* (Slave Labor Graphics, 2004). A high school student discovers her own conscience and moral compass when she dreams of a saint who has lost his faith. Yang works effectively in black ink, showing Loyola working through her understanding of human salvation. Ⓔ

MYTHS, LEGENDS, AND FOLKTALES

McCulloch, Derek, and Shepherd Hendrix. *Stagger Lee* (Image Comics, 2006). The American pop song has its roots in a tale that has been told and reconstituted for over a century. Here, both art and text document the assorted facts, probable underpinnings, and variety of renditions of how Lee Shelton came to kill Billy Lyons in that Wild West barroom.

Medley, Linda. *Castle Waiting* (Fantagraphics, 2006). The fractured fairy tale derives increased value when seen as well as narrated. Here, there's room for feminism and modern appliances in a realm that is populated by large talking birds, plus beautiful women and fat men, in full, clear-line color.

Messner-Loebs, William, and Sam Keith. *Epicurus: The Sage* (Wildstorm, 2003). Plato, Alexander the Great, and Epicurus coexist here to the benefit of those who wonder how some great ideas were developed and what might have happened along the way (but probably didn't). Color and black-and-white images both have roles in the visual content, just as both verbal disputation and physical humor come to the fore to express the myth behind history and the reality underpinning mythology. Ⓔ

✱ ↔ Sen, Jai, and Rizky Wasisto Edi. *Garlands of Moonlight* (Shoto Press, 2002). A Malaysian folktale of a village haunted by a mysterious plague becomes fully realized in this small but gem-like production in which black-and-white ink is coated with silver. The pages literally shimmer and make the highly individualized characters appear to be realistically ethereal. See also the sequel, *The Ghost of Silver Cliff* (Shoto Press, 2002).

✤ Sen, Jai, Seijuro Mizu, Umeka Asayuki, and Shino Yotsumoto. *The Golden Vine* (Shoto Press, 2003). In this version of ancient history, Alexander the Great was able to unite the known world. The tale unfolds in three parts, each drawn by a different artist but each employing black ink images that are overlaid with gold, highly appropriate both to the traditional story and this alternative.

✤ ↔ Shanower, Eric. Age of Bronze series (Image Comics, 2001–). While the author intends to report the details of the Trojan War in an estimated seven volumes, only half of them are complete at this time. Fully and carefully researched, the presentation interweaves history with mythology, provides accurate and detailed pictures of clothing, hairstyles, and architecture, and moves forward as the Greek myths do, which is not with the chronological obsession textbooks provide. Ⓔ

✤ ↔ Sheinkin, Steve. *The Wit and Wisdom of Rabbi Harvey* (Jewish Lights Publishing, 2006). Sepia-washed cartoons fit well with the time, place, and tenor of these Jewish folktales by way of nineteenth-century Colorado. The rabbi plays the traditional folklore role of wise and witty intercessor in mundane dilemmas, while the settings and set-ups are distinctly American folkloric. There's more of this in *Rabbi Harvey Rides Again* (Jewish Lights Publishing, 2008).

✤ ↔ Yang, Gene Luen. *American Born Chinese* (First Second, 2006). A story of an Asian American boy's quest for identity and belonging is tightly woven into a retelling of the traditional Monkey King trickster tale. Color is employed symbolically as well as realistically in the clear-line cartoons that depict racial stereotypes through the protagonist's eyes. Ⓔ

HEALTH AND WELLNESS

↔ Lay, Carol. *The Big Skinny: How I Changed My Fattitude* (Villard, 2008). While the diet and exercise advice provided here is gimmickless common sense, Lay's willingness to show as well as tell how she followed the rules and how she changed appearance and energy level in the process are inspired and inspiring. The cartoony images bring an appeal and bounce even to such discursive passages as how to properly measure ingredients.

Peeters, Frederik. *Blue Pills: A Positive Love Story* (Houghton Mifflin, 2008). A casual relationship with a young woman who is HIV positive—and the mother of an HIV positive toddler—turns to love in this autobiographical account. Peeters uses delightful and unexpected symbolism to show how the couple confronts current reality and HIV's changing prognosis. (T)

↔ Pekar, Harvey, Joyce Brabner, and Frank Stack. *Our Cancer Year* (Four Walls Eight Windows, 1994). Comics legend Pekar and his wife lay bare the physical and emotional devastation caused by his lymphoma, and their ultimate survival of this event. Black-and-white images convey body language as well as facial expression and bring this very real account into fully furnished and landscaped awareness. (E)

Tobe, Keiko. *With the Light: Raising an Autistic Child* (Yen Press, 2007–2009). In five translated volumes, the social, familial, and educational complexities of the title subject are explored through the lens of one particular family. Copious amounts of advice, theories, and best practices are made accessible through storytelling that shows as well as narrates. Everything in this manga presentation is translated here, including signage and T-shirt slogans. (T)

✳ Winick, Judd. *Pedro and Me: Friendship, Loss, and What I Learned* (Henry Holt, 2000). In addition to exploring AIDS and AIDS education as it was offered to youth fifteen years ago, Winick also shares how friendship and loss gave him the storytelling voice and need his cartooning craft required to move from technique to art. The multicultural cast of characters is presented with each one's unique features and speech patterns. (E)

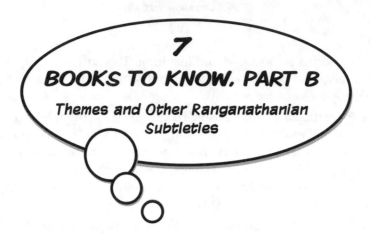

7

BOOKS TO KNOW, PART B

Themes and Other Ranganathanian Subtleties

Not all readers place prime importance on the obvious topics of the books they favor. The experienced readers' advisor has worked with clients whose interest is piqued by reading that offers difficulty or simplicity, specific values, engagement through emotional or intellectual appeal, and other, more subtle attributes than topic, genre, or plot. Identifying such concerns can be of great help in finding the right book for the right reader at the right time.

PUSHING THE FORMAT BOUNDARIES

With graphic novels being the specific format, the following suggestions are arranged by engagement qualities other than genre, plot, or topic as titles were enumerated in the previous chapter. This chapter offers starting points, or examples, of reading choices that have graphic novel qualities expressed in ways that bring the specific titles to the edges of the format. We'll start with picture stories that are wordless and move through to single works in which sequential art shares space with other narrative formatting to create a unified whole.

As in the previous chapter, the titles included in this chapter serve more as example than as a suggested canon. To that end, some entries include discussions rather than annotations. The same caveat holds as in chapter 6: a list proffered to the client inquiring after reading advice is no substitute for the conversation that can help that potential reader identify which book best serves her in this moment.

The following are the codes appear at the head of relevant entries and are used to denote suggested audiences:

✣ appropriate for younger readers (under sixteen in some communities, as young as under twelve in others)

↔ crossover title for readers unfamiliar with the format

The following codes appear at the end of the annotation for relevant
titles, and denote publishing contexts:

Ⓔ instance of work by creator(s) with an extensive body of published
sequential art including other graphic novels, comics, cartoons, or
a combination of these formats

Ⓣ English language edition is a translation

WORDLESS FICTION

Whether a truly wordless narrative is a graphic novel may be debatable,
given the definition of a graphic novel as a narrative in which text and
image interplay to create a whole. Certainly most image-only works are
not graphic novels. The ones listed here, however, each have an inten-
tional order and require the reader to bring a literate frame to moving
from image to image. These are images that are read and in reading allow
a specific story, with plot, character, and themes, to appear.

Publication information here refers to currently available editions.
Several of the titles listed are more than fifty years old, clearly predating
the concept of graphic novel.

✣ Banyai, Istvan. *Zoom* (Viking, 1995). Full-page frames push the reader
farther and farther from the scene as it appears to morph from one
image detail to a very different organizing image. Barnyard? Cruise
ship? Postage stamp? See also the sequel, *Re-zoom* (Viking, 1995). Ⓔ

Drooker, Eric. *Blood Song: A Silent Ballad* (Harcourt, 2002). Escaping war
in Asia and eventually finding peace, and perhaps love, in the West,
the young woman at the heart of this adventure must cope with both
physical and emotional storms. Color-washed scratchboard and block
printing are both used, sometimes in monochrome and sometimes
more diversely hued, and the story moves between expression in full-
page images and small panels. See also Drooker's *Flood!* (Dark Horse,
2002). Ⓔ

Hartzell, Andy. *Fox Bunny Funny* (Top Shelf Productions, 2007). In three
acts, a tale of identity and public revelation of it unfolds. A fox

would have preferred to be a bunny and, in expressive black ink on bright white ground, pursues that in the face of peer and parental pressures.

Kuper, Peter. *Sticks and Stones* (Three Rivers, 2004). An allegory of war and peace is revealed as a stone giant enforces fealty among a group of people and demands their attack on a neighboring group. The full-color art is spray paint over lines created with stencils. See also Kuper's collections of brief wordless stories and visual puzzles in *The Eye of the Beholder* (NBM, 2006) and other titles. Ⓔ

Masereel, Frans. *Passionate Journey* (Dover, 2007). Sometimes credited as the founder of wordless literature, the artist presents his story through woodcuts: the then-modern European intellectual is shown through a singular man as he explores both external and interior aspects of life. This was first published around 1920, and was followed by more than a dozen others by this author as well as by European and American peers. Ⓔ Ⓣ

Nückel, Otto. *Destiny* (Dover, 2007). Among the earliest modern published narratives relying on image rather than word as conveyor of plot, character, and meaning, the block prints, here created with lead, tell the story of a woman whose lot in life seems to be to move from one misfortune to another. This was originally published in Germany in 1930. Ⓣ

✳ Tan, Shaun. *The Arrival* (Arthur A. Levine Books, 2007). Large pages hold tiny penciled panels or full-page scenes, most washed in sepia, that document an immigrant's arrival with all the associated wonders, regrets, and surprises that that experience entails. Tan also creates graphic novel stories with a few words, like *Tales from Outer Suburbia* (Templar Publishing, 2009).

Ward, Lynd. *Mad Man's Drum* (Dover, 2005). Block prints from woodcuts, each on its own page, tell a psychologically terrifying story. The author, working in the United States less than a generation after Masereel and Nückel (above) were active in Europe, wrote many wordless books for adults, some for children (*The Silver Pony*, Houghton Mifflin, 1973), and illustrated picture books with text as well (*The Biggest Bear*, Houghton Mifflin, 1952). Ⓔ

ADAPTATIONS FROM TEXT TO SEQUENTIAL ART NARRATIVE

Unlike the old Classics Illustrated series of half a century ago, these adaptations are the products of individual artists working on individually chosen literary projects. For both the adapters and the reader, celebration of the original work, rather than replacement of it, lie at the core. Readers with visual preferences will find these adaptations pleasing while more auditory prose readers may find themselves slowed by the process of looking deeply, a slowing that can be helpful to their appreciation of the story or frustrating, depending on the individual and the time at which she comes to the adaptation.

Auster, Paul, Paul Karasik, and David Mazzucchelli. *City of Glass* (Picador, 2004). The existential novella is simplified without being made simplistic, so that it can be delivered through sharply black-and-white images. Some are flat cartoons while others mere sketches, just as the original work moved between something close to reality and a much less stable state of mind.

✱ Carey, Mike, and Glenn Fabry. *Neil Gaiman's Neverwhere* (DC Comics, Vertigo, 2007). The comics-friendly novelist lends his story of identity and betrayal, with the city of London itself featured as the underworld, to full-color treatment that shows the horror of foiled attempts to escape oblivion. The natural and unnatural worlds are both depicted to suspenseful and evocative effect. **(E)**

✱ Dixon, Charles, David Wenzel, and J. R. R. Tolkien. *The Hobbit: An Illustrated Edition of the Fantasy Classic* (Ballantine, 1990). Painterly scenes bring rich visual life to the fantasy story of Bilbo Baggins. The abridgement is profound in that it leaves a satisfying short story for readers to enjoy. **(E)**

Eisner, Will. *Fagin the Jew* (Doubleday, 2003). In addition to creating original stories and expository texts on the sequential art craft, Eisner adapted a number of stories by canonical authors. Unlike most of the titles and efforts mentioned in the rest of this section, Eisner typically selected a single character from the original work and presented just a few details from the author's text through a new lens, the lens of the selected character. Here then, in shaded pencil and with Victorian details apparent in architecture and postures, is an aspect of Charles Dickens's *Oliver Twist* told through the eyes of one of the novel's archetypal bad guys. **(E)**

❊ Heuet, Stéphane, and Marcel Proust. *Remembrance of Things Past* (NBM, ComicsLit, 2001–). In a work that is to expand to about a dozen volumes in English, Proust's moody and period-drenched study of personal memory is interpreted in clear line style that fits plot and mood like a glove. The narration retains Proust's voice while the expressive characters appear just as he described them. Ⓔ Ⓣ

↔ Jacobson, Sid, and Ernie Colon. *The 9/11 Report: A Graphic Adaptation* (Hill and Wang, 2006). The U.S.-government-published report on the mechanics and political diagnosis of this event are presented through sequential art that breathes accessibility into the original. Full-color and carefully arranged panels provide information that cannot be so well-documented in prose, such as the simultaneity of the airline disasters and racial profiling in the aftermath. The sequel, *After 9/11: America's War on Terrorism, 2001–* (Hill and Wang, 2008), discusses political and related cultural events that have occurred in the wake of this watershed day. Ⓔ

↔ King, Stephen, Peter David, and others. *The Dark Tower* (Marvel Comics, 2007–). The Midworld horror series is reconceived as a satisfying series of graphic novels painted by Jae Lee in a palette of bright colors. Close-ups and vistas are both employed to dramatic effect.

↔ Kuper, Peter, and Franz Kafka. *The Metamorphosis* (Crown, 2003). In a heavy ink style that emulates woodblock printing, the story of man-turned-insect is recapitulated, this time with the viewpoint of the narrative shared between the poor fellow and his sister. The turn-of-the-century German setting is depicted through furnishings as well as period symbolism. See also Kuper's adaptation of Upton Sinclair's *The Jungle* (NBM, 1991), which is in full and appropriately lurid color. Ⓔ

Lark, Michael, and Alex Wald. *Raymond Chandler's Philip Marlowe: The Little Sister* (Fireside, 1997). Retaining some of the noir detective author's text and giving it period-piece-looking visuals, this is one of several efforts to move Chandler into graphic novel form. While *The Little Sister* was published by Chandler as a novel (Hamish Hamilton, 1949), there's also a graphic novel treatment of an unproduced Chandler film script—Françoise Ayroles and Ted Benoit's *Playback* (Arcade Publishing, 2006)—which the adapters translated into French and which was then translated back into English for its American publication.

Parks, Ande, and Chris Samnee. *Capote in Kansas* (Oni Press, 2005). Truman Capote's research for his nonfiction novel *In Cold Blood* (Modern Library, 2002) is shown here in densely shaded black ink panels that depict events from just beyond Capote's own view and include the on-the-ground work provided by Harper Lee as it was never acknowledged in his own publication. Ⓔ

✲ Petrucha, Stefan, and Kody Chamberlain. *Beowulf* (HarperCollins, 2007). Murky hues and minimal dialogue are used to good effect to retell the story of Grendel and his mother. While the language of the classic is missing here, the images help to set the scene for a fuller reading of the poem.

✲ ↔ Plessix, Michel, and Kenneth Grahame. *The Wind in the Willows* (NBM, 2001–). Highly detailed but tiny panels allow the story of Ratty and Toad to unfold in bright colors and with a plethora of active postures and mood-telegraphing expressions. Backdrops are busy with mechanical and natural sounds rendered in shaped and colored text, while the foreground often appears at nearly hallucinatory angles.

✲ Shanower, Eric. *Adventures in Oz* (IDW, 2006). Shanower has been adapting various stories from L. Frank Baum's Oz cycle for more than two decades. Each one is large, highly detailed, and painted with a glowing palette. Renderings of the cast have them appearing as they might in Baum's lifetime, rather than as more rounded modern cartoon caricatures. Ⓔ

✲ Siku. *Manga Bible* (Galilee Trade, 2008). Stories from both the Old and New Testaments, with appropriate cross-references to specific books and verses, are interpreted resonantly. Modern dress and idiom from a variety of cultures appear in some, while others have a more traditional look and sound. Ⓔ

Van den Bogaert, H. M., and George O'Connor. *Journey into Mohawk Country* (First Second, 2006). The diary maintained by a seventeenth-century explorer is visualized by a modern cartoonist. Pages tend to one bold color or another, as firelight, snow, and the more metaphoric darkness or brightness of dread or hope provide the setting of the immediate passage. Ⓣ

✲ Yang, Gene Luen. *The Rosary Comic Book* (Slave Labor Graphics, 2004). The prayer cycles associated with the rosary are reconstituted in full, but with the rosary beads replaced by respectful images of relevant persons and events. Ⓔ

SERIES WITH STAND-ALONE TITLES

Unlike the serial comic book, graphic novels can belong to an ongoing series in which each volume can stand complete and understood by itself. Some authors employ a stable of characters in a variety of independently rendered adventures, while others create independent stories or nonfiction accounts that share a central theme across a collection of titles. Readers who appreciate the reliability of the tried-and-true may feel most comfortable reading a series, knowing that each title in it will have something in common with one read and appreciated previously.

Publication dates listed for these refer to current editions.

Geary, Rick. A Treasury of Victorian Murder (NBM, 1987–2007). Each volume explores a specific historic crime, including the yet unsolved cases attributed to Jack the Ripper, accused but unconvicted patricide Lizzie Borden, and H. H. Holmes, memorialized as the serial killer at the Chicago World's Fair. Other cases look at presidential assassinations where the killer has been identified with forensic certainty. Black ink drawings, with lots of period detail and perspectives that hew close to the Victorian aesthetic, show the facts, including maps and building layouts, trials, and crime scene discoveries. In each case, Geary has provided references to the materials he used to research the story and in each case he provides a comprehensive and accessible overview of the crime and the ambiguities that may remain around its solution. (E)

✳ Goscinny, René, and Albert Uderzo. Asterix (Orion, 2004–). The adventures of a cartoon Gaul and his buddies—including one who is an anachronistic riff on Shakespeare—take the Roman Empire by storm in a series of geographically specific adventures that include trips to Belgium and Corsica, and causes that range from battling slavery to competing in the Olympics. Highly colored clear line cartoons, with lots of puns and some real history, combine to make these timeless in their appeal. (E) (T)

✳ Hergé. The Adventures of Tintin (Little, Brown, 2008). The boy reporter created between the world wars as an intrepid explorer has seen lots of translations and some rewriting of early, pro-colonial episodes. Tintin travels to Scotland, the Himalayas, and Egypt, among other places. Hergé is touted as the premier clear line cartoonist, but he also concocts clever puns that survive nicely in translation. A variety of book formats are available, including volumes in which multiple tales are bound together and paperback volumes of individual stories. Ⓔ Ⓣ

Pomplun, Tom, editor. Graphic Classics (Eureka, 2006–). In its second edition of publication, this long-running and engaging series is composed of black-and-white volumes, each of which is dedicated to a particular author or genre. As many as ten cartoonists work on each, interpreting the words of the original author's poems, short stories, or parts of novels as true graphic novel pieces. The range of authors so treated includes Edgar Allan Poe, Mark Twain, O. Henry, and Jane Austen. Artists working on portions of this series include Rick Geary, Tom Neely, Peter Kuper, Spain Rodriguez, and dozens more. Ⓔ

INSTRUCTION THROUGH SEQUENTIAL ART

During World War II, Will Eisner spent his time in the U.S. Army creating instructional material in sequential art format. Some topics are particularly receptive to this presentation—and some readers find such access a welcome respite from trying to decode manuals or follow oral instructions.

The books listed here serve as examples of such instructional treatment. Unlike the subjects detailed in chapter 6, publishing has been less reliable in offering expansive examples of this type of graphic novelization of content. Specific titles come and go, often providing explanations for concerns that become dated either in interest or specific details of the sequential art interpretations.

Gonick, Larry. *The Cartoon Guide to (Non-) Communication: The Use and Misuse of Information in the Modern World* (HarperPerennial, 1993). An inspired choice of subject matter from the cartoonist who also presents various science and history topics through black-and-white cartoons and incisive facts, this book shows what doesn't work when we try to reach each other. Given how modern communication has changed—both technically and in effect—the actual instruction here is less immediately descriptive and more of a beginning point for exploring information exchanges in the twenty-first century. Gonick's style, both artistic and analytic, is a model for instructional sequential art texts. Ⓔ

Lencioni, Patrick, and Kensuke Okabayashi. *Five Dysfunctions of a Team* (Wiley, 2008). Standard business literature meets manga, and the sum is greater than the parts. Because the images show emotion simultaneous with discussions of the how and why of emotions' causation and organizational effects, the presentation becomes experiential rather than clinical. Business topics occasionally receive such sequential art treatment, often to excellent effect, but the effort hasn't been sustained enough in the United States to produce a reliable body of options for self-help business readers.

Lurio, Eric. *The Cartoon Guide to the Constitution of the United States* (Barnes and Noble Books, 1987). Although there is some editorializing here, the thrust of the commentary that accompanies the full text of the Constitution is explanatory and contextual. The sequential art is done with an eye toward humor as well as exposition of the document. This has a longer shelf life than similar treatments of economics or technology.

Takahashi, Shin. *Manga Guide to Statistics* (No Starch Press, 2008). One in a new series by the publisher, this guide's approach is thorough and accessible. Ad-Manga, the company that provides important design aspects for these texts, is a studio providing art to manga writers. In this way, the work differs from Larry Gonick's personal and personalized approach. (See above.) Also different from Gonick's take on similar topics, the books in this series offer stories in which the instruction is couched, rather than addressing the reader more directly. Other titles in this very current series treat calculus, electricity, and other tech-oriented fields of inquiry.

SHORTS

Essays and short story anthologies hold appeal to some readers, whether they want only a brief experiment with the format or simply prefer, more generally, shorter narrative arcs.

Brunetti, Ivan, editor. *An Anthology of Graphic Fiction, Cartoons, and True Stories* (Yale University Press, 2006). Both well-known and relatively obscure but equally excellent artists are brought to attention in a collection of significant short pieces. As well as offering a large number of contributors, there is a wide range of styles and conceptual approaches. Some pieces here are panel cartoons, rather than narratives. A second volume with the same title followed in 2008. Ⓔ

Burford, Brendan, editor. *Syncopated: An Anthology of Nonfiction Picto-Essays* (Villard, 2009). A wide assortment of topics, each engagingly and informatively presented, is brought together: subway art history, developmental psychology, and hay baling to name a few. An equally diverse assortment of black-and-white visual styles, including silhouette and pen sketching, show the possibilities and flexibility of the format. Each of the pieces is the work of a different artist or writer-artist team.

Collier, David. *Just the Facts: A Decade of Comics Essays* (Drawn and Quarterly, 1998). These pieces all come from a single creator but cover a range of brief sequential art pieces arranged by broad topics—nostalgia, sports, and travel among them. Here the shaded black-and-white images are all presented in small panels, many with lots of text. The pieces are quite brief, some only a dozen panels.

Ilya (Ed Hillyer), editor. *The Mammoth Book of Best New Manga* (Running Press, 2007–). Full-color production of pieces from many countries showcase the many styles and conventions that make up manga and how manga can be used to create stories in many genres. There are a few explanations of forms and story types included in each annual volume.

✳ Kibuishi, Kazu, editor. *Flight Explorer* (Villard, 2008–). This annual anthology of short sequential art stories offers youth the kind of eclectic opportunity that the annual anthology *Flight* (Villard, 2007–) offers adults. A variety of genres, as well as narrative and artistic styles, are presented, all high quality and capable of giving readers a taste of the format's potential. The artists showcased work in related fields, including animation and color production, as well as some who are primarily sequential art storytellers.

Modan, Rutu. *Jamilti and Other Stories* (Drawn and Quarterly, 2008). In this collection of full-color stories, the Israeli artist explores various settings and themes, including the folkloric, politics in the Middle East, and personal disappointment. Each story is completely formed and different in plot from the rest, while the blocky images remain a constant. ⓣ

Murphy, Mark. *House of Java* (NBM, 1998). The sometime customers of a Seattle coffee shop each play the main character in a short story here: a teenage girl pursues her wandering boyfriend, local college students hang out, an elderly man seems to have nowhere else as hopeful to go. The black-and-white art is evocative of suburban plainness. See also volume 2, which carries the same title (2002), and in which the settings deviate more often from the original coffee shop interior.

↔ Rodriguez, Jason, editor. *Postcards: True Stories That Never Happened* (Villard, 2007). Postcards selected and written years ago, and then found at jumble sales, provided the sparks for more than a dozen brief sequential art stories from as many artists. This concept manages to weave together fact and fiction, images of historic documents, and imagined backstories for an eclectic but unified visual tour of possible moments. Individual drawing styles further the tone and visual themes selected to convey each narrative.

Wertz, Julia, editor. *I Saw You . . . Comics Inspired by Real-Life Missed Connections* (Three Rivers, 2009). A number of currently active American cartoonists contributed their interpretations of personal ad "missed opportunities" that span the bittersweet to the desperate. Style and quality of the visual art varies, as do the voices the creators use to recreate these missed liaisons.

AND HERE THE LINE BLURS: MULTIFORMAT

Instead of winding text and image together, some authors and artists present their work in a variety of formats, each expressing an essential part of the narrative. Such works require the reader to bring different kinds of information gathered in different moments together, a cerebral exercise that won't appeal to all but which has high appeal to others.

In addition to books in which the artist has made use of varying visual approaches—collage and photo as well as comics panels, for instance—noted here, too, are books of sequential art that have beginning, middle, and end points forming a story arc, but which are composed of comic strips that formed the story originally over a period of series publication. In some cases, the "graphic novel" lives online, having been printed from beginning to end as a series, but not yet available in book format.

Batiuk, Tom. *Lisa's Story: The Other Shoe* (Kent State University Press, 2007). The strip cartoonist's daily, Funky Winkerbean, has had two story arcs presenting a character's battle with breast cancer. The relevant strips are collected here to form a whole story. The pacing differs from a work conceived as a graphic novel, or even a collection of sequential art short pieces, but character development and plot resonate and the images and text are essential partners in the storytelling.

↔ Guibert, Emmanuel. *The Photographer* (First Second, 2009). A trip with Doctors Without Borders, undertaken by photographer Didier Lefevre in the mid-1980s, is recapitulated through a fully colored sequential art narrative interspersed—illustrated, as it were—with Lefevre's mostly black-and-white photos. The result is part journalism, part autobiography, and all visually and intellectually compelling. Ⓔ Ⓣ

Niffenegger, Audrey. *The Night Bookmobile* (www.guardian.co.uk/books/ 2008/may/31/nightbookmobile/). Published in weekly installments in the Manchester (U.K.) *Guardian*, this story of affection for books and serving potential readers is available page by page across its thirty-two installments. The full-color graphic novel will be published in Britain late in 2009. This same newspaper and its online site presented readers with Posy Simmonds's graphic novel *Tamara Drewe* (Houghton Mifflin, 2008) before it was published in book format. Look to the site for future graphic novels in web format.

Osborne, Richard, and Ralph Edney. *Philosophy for Beginners* (Writers and Readers, 2007). Sequential art spreads, illustrations of concepts and maps, and paragraphs in straight text allow the reader to graze from idea to explanation. This title is one in a lengthy series of black-and-white books, each treating a discipline or famous figure from history, science, philosophy, or literature. The presentation here mimics in print the mental workings of a first serious personal consideration of the topic.

Rall, Ted. *Silk Road to Ruin* (NBM, 2006). In addition to working as a cartoonist, Rall is a "thrill tourist" who regularly challenges himself by traveling to international hot spots. Collected here are his adventures in the Middle East, as lived across a decade or more of travels. He uses straight text, illustration, photographs, and sequential art to present different aspects of his observations and reports.

✳ Selznick, Brian. *The Invention of Hugo Cabret* (Scholastic Press, 2007). In order to read this story, it's necessary to interpret passages that are visual and others that are text. Rather than appearing together, the adventure of a boy discovering a world hidden by complex mechanical things unfolds in alternating formats. The art is black-and-white sketchwork, sometimes busy and sometimes as simple as a posture detail. Ⓔ

Talbot, Bryan. *Alice in Sunderland* (Dark Horse, 2007). Metafiction meets meta-art in this collage of literary and popular cultural explorations that segues from autobiography to satire. Talbot interweaves the town of Sunderland as well as the myth and the rumors that remake Alice Liddell even now, one hundred and fifty years after Lewis Carroll placed her as the star in his fantasy stories, and the different forces of ink, photography, computer-generated imagery, and paint, used together and distinctly.

WHAT'S NEXT ...

In the following chapter, more resources for identifying graphic novels for your readers are discussed. But track your own resources as well: the artists your advice seekers note, reviews of new titles that appear in the "civilian" as well as professional review presses, and your own gems discovered while browsing.

There is no end to a readers' advisory education, but here's to an organized beginning!

8

PROFESSIONAL TOOLS

Bibliographies, Webliographies, and Guides for the Advisor

Keeping abreast of all the new releases in the field of graphic novels, comic books, and sequential art is both essential and daunting for the practicing advisor. In order to have the widest array of options at the ready, a practitioner necessarily relies on the research and analyses others conduct by way of reviews, guidebooks, professional and fan websites dedicated to the format, and annotated, thematic lists that can be only as exhaustive as their publication dates allow.

This chapter will discuss the best of these resources that are available as of the time of this book's publication. The advisor will need to find even newer resources as soon this list is considered. But, as with many bibliographic essays, what is mentioned here should continue to be useful as a beginning point even as it fails to reach into every successive future moment.

ANNOTATED GENERAL BIBLIOGRAPHIES

Print Format

These two titles are essential for the readers' advisor's active reference shelf and as references for collection building and maintenance:

D. Aviva Rothschild published *Graphic Novels: A Bibliographic Guide to Book-Length Comics* nearly fifteen years ago, but it continues to offer a model not only of fine selection but also of fair, detailed, and helpful annotating.[1] A readers' advisor who is new to working with readers and sequential art should look here to identify core classic titles and to learn the essential details an advisor should highlight when introducing titles to potential readers.

Gene Kannenberg Jr.'s *500 Essential Graphic Novels: The Ultimate Guide* provides well-conceived details as well, with titles divided into ten broad appeal categories and each title described in terms of plot and read-alikes.[2] While Rothschild's book is text-only, Kannenberg's includes accurately reprinted sample pages. Rothschild's annotations are lengthier, but both provide multiple indexing and a range of titles for a range of reader ages and tastes.

While Kannenberg shows the art a reader can expect from each title, Rothschild uses rich vocabulary and prose to communicate the qualities of each book. Both means of providing information are essential to the readers' advisor who is trying to present visual literature through verbal communication.

The Rough Guide to Graphic Novels, edited by Danny Fingeroth, provides readers with an advisory tool that's just bigger than pocket-sized.[3] Sixty "literary" graphic novels are described and illustrated, but there are also read-alike lists and a good introduction to the medium and its history. Biographies and online resources are noted throughout. This title belongs in library collections for readers to borrow so they can browse as fully as they like, although it is also a suitable collection-building tool for libraries.

Graphic Novels: A Genre Guide to Comic Books, Manga, and More by librarian Michael Pawuk lists twenty-four hundred titles and provides indexing by character as well as by creator and subject.[4] An excellent collection development tool, this one will be popular with dedicated comics readers and can help catalogers and social catalog taggers to provide context for listings of what the library owns.

Online

Finding annotated bibliographies on the Web—covering any format, genre, or taste known to readerkind—can be as easy as typing the request into Google. However, knowing which websites provide exhaustive, well-annotated, and helpful suggestions to the readers' advisor takes a bit more finesse.

Knowing which agencies are likely to keep their online lists updated is a start. Websites maintained by some publishers, some libraries, and some fans are good starting points. In the case of graphic novel publishers, coverage will, of course, be limited to titles produced by the host company. However, these can offer rich information for any advisor who may not be able to have first-hand experience with every graphic novel currently available. Larger publishers—but some independent ones as well—offer sample pages online, as well as verbal descriptions of title content and pointers to other titles by their authors.

Subscription Database

To date, the only significant entry here is H. W. Wilson's Graphic Novels Core Collection, which provides libraries, especially those working with youth, a reliably updated access point to professionally reviewed titles. The database allows searching by subject and genre, helpful aids to the readers' advisor.

Book Publishers That Maintain Strong Online Lists

Drawn and Quarterly (www.drawnandquarterly.com/artHome.php) organizes by artist, with each link providing previews, biography, and catalog of the artist's in-house titles.

First Second: The Collection (www.firstsecondbooks.com/collection .html) provides access to excerpts, hyperlinked annotations, and editorial reviews, with separate lists for younger and mature readers.

NBM Publishing (www.nbmpub.com/index.html) provides several portals to annotated lists of its publications, including series in the ComicsLit imprint, mystery, fantasy/sci-fi/horror, and humor and classics; each title annotation includes narrative, editorial review snips, and preview pages.

Pantheon Graphic Novels (www.randomhouse.com/pantheon/ graphicnovels/home.pperl) offers information about authors and titles of the adult graphic novels from the publisher who first brought Art Spiegelman's *Maus* to readers in book format.[5]

Vertigo (www.dccomics.com/graphic_novels/?cat=VERTIGO) offers an online catalog, presented in alphabetical order by title, which includes cover images, occasional page previews, and annotations that offer readers an accurate overview of storyline and appeal characteristics.

Bookstores and Libraries

A number of American libraries and bookstores have created online graphic novel lists. While other such reader services outlets may bring graphic novels into occasional focus, the following have a track record of maintaining the focus and keeping their online annotated lists up to date:

Powell's Books (www.powells.com/subsection/GraphicNovelsGener al.html) offers both peer-to-peer and expert opinion, as it features reader annotations as well as providing staff written synopses and reviews.

Get Graphic: The World in Words and Pictures (www.getgraphic .org) provides a dynamic portal to lists, fan sites, creator sites, and library programming that calls on youth to participate in sequential art literacy and culture.

State Library of Tasmania (www.statelibrary.tas.gov.au/readrelax/ graphicnovels/) provides depth and flexible access to annotated lists of graphic novels, as well as a staff-written blog updating the basic lists.

Blogs and Independent Websites

Providing meatier content than fan sites, the authors of the following are professional critics, readers, and advisors.

Comics Worth Reading: Graphic Novels (http://comicsworthreading .com/category/graphic-novels/). Johanna Draper Carlson offers annotations with appeal elements spelled out, as well as hyperlinks to titles related in content, authorship, or style.

¡*Journalista!* (www.tcj.com/journalista/). *The Comics Journal's* Dirk Deppey provides generous links to both editors and sequential art creators from his blog.

No Flying, No Tights (www.noflyingnotights.com). Robin Brenner provides three age-specific annotated lists and has long been trusted as the friend of youth librarians new to graphic novel advisory work.

BEYOND GENERAL LISTS

Locating and researching annotated lists provides the readers' advisor with specific titles to forward to readers. But in order to continue to grow an understanding of both the appeal and evolution of the format, professional reading beyond lists should be on the advisor's roster of goals and objectives. The titles discussed in this section provide professional development material for advisors, whether or not they are able to continue to expand their background and understanding of the format through more active instruction, conference attendance, and other suggested means of updating professional skills. They are not suggested as replacements for such active participation in groups convened to examine graphic novels as reading material.

Monographs

Scott McCloud's three books on comics are required reading for any readers' advisor who needs a thorough understanding of the mechanics of sequential art. *Understanding Comics: The Invisible Art* and *Making Comics: Storytelling Secrets of Comics, Manga and Graphic Novels* provide fine studies of the rhetoric of sequential art.[6] *Reinventing Comics: How Imagination and Technology Are Revolutionizing an Art Form* is a discourse on sequential art's difficulties with staying abreast of social evolution and a forecast of the role the Internet could—and did—come to play in sequential art publishing and reader access. All three volumes are written in sequential art format.[7]

A pair of recent and more scholarly examinations of comics each includes insights for the advisor who wants to broaden his or her critical understanding of the format. *The Language of Comics: Word and Image,* edited by Robin Varnum and Christina Gibbons, comprises ten essays broaching topics from sound sense in Asterix to wordless narrative as exemplified by Peter Kuper and Eric Drooker.[8] Rocco Versaci's *This Book Contains Graphic Language: Comics as Literature* examines graphic novels specifically under a sociopolitical lens, concentrating on memoir, journalism, and cultural exegesis.[9]

How-to books for cartoonists can also provide readers' advisors with fresh ways of describing graphic novels and/or analyzing appeal aspects. Will Eisner's *Comics and Sequential Art* and *Graphic Storytelling and Visual Narrative;* Chris Hart's how-to books including *Drawing Crime Noir* and *Manga Mania;* and Bob Pendarvis and Mark Kneece's *Bristol Board Jungle* each contribute to a broad-based understanding of how sequential art "works" for both writer and reader.[10] Eisner's two volumes are textbooks for adult students. Hart's books are intended for the beginner. Pendarvis and Kneece have published the result of an art school classroom exercise in presenting the making of a graphic novel through a graphic novel format narrative.

Some seemingly specialized titles also offer the graphic novel readers' advisor information and inspiration that can improve his or her general knowledge of the format. Klaus Janson's *The DC Comics Guide to Pencilling Comics* gives an overview of storytelling with sequential art that is accessible and enlightening to critics as well as novices.[11] Matt Madden's *99 Ways to Tell a Story* shows how the distinguishing characteristics of style, viewpoint, and a balance between text and image alter, enhance, or detract from a sequential art scene.[12]

The Librarian's Guide to Graphic Novels for Children and Tweens by David S. Serchay is indispensable to advisors working with the title populations.[13] In addition to its annotated and helpfully categorized lists that suggest books in typical genre and appeal categories, it includes discussions and suggestions of representative titles addressing ethnic and gender diversity, adaptations of other media including related traditional print books, and display ideas that speak to readers' advisory concerns. Serchay's discussions of developmental issues of the juvenile reader are insightful and well serve both the children's specialist who is not yet comfortable with graphic novels, and the generalist advisor who may need better acquaintance with the age group to serve children well.

Other books targeting specialized readers' advisory practices are Robin Brenner's *Understanding Manga and Anime* and Stephen Cary's *Going Graphic: Comics at Work in the Multilingual Classroom.*[14] Both titles direct the reader to consider theoretical aspects of sequential art but also provide title suggestions and activities that can be adapted by readers' advisors in search of extending services into the realm of formal programming.

Journals

Serials dedicated to collection development as well as to comics format criticism provide ongoing assistance to the advisor who wants to keep up to date on what's available and how new titles share appeal with earlier titles. Most are available in both print and online venues. Among those most important for the active advisor to maintain as current reference material are

Booklist	*Publisher's Weekly*
Library Journal	*The Comics Journal*

Websites

Beyond reviews and articles offering what seem to be straightforward reading suggestions, a range of sites created by both professionals and fans offer the advisor additional tools. Among the best are

Diamond Bookshelf (www.diamondbookshelf.com/public/). Although highly commercial, this distributor's site includes lists, essays by scholars and readers' services practitioners, and related content that speaks to advisors' ongoing need for up-to-date market information.

GraphicNovelReporter (http://graphicnovelreporter.com). Published by *The Book Report,* this portal gives access to opinion pieces as well as reviews, interviews, and relevant blogs.

ImageText: Interdisciplinary Comics Studies (www.english.ufl.edu/ imagetext/). Published since 2004, this scholarly journal provides about ten theme-specific articles per issue, addressing such topics as "William Blake and Visual Culture," aesthetics, and Neil Gaiman.

More Than 100 Comics-Related Words in 8 Languages (http://lefevre .pascal.googlepages.com/morethan100comics-relatedwordsin 8languag). While it's not likely that American advisors need ready access to Dutch or Portuguese terms for describing aspects of sequential art narrative, this list (which is arranged alphabetically in English) is an excellent introduction to the terminology that an advisor has at the ready.

AWARDS

Among book awards highlighting graphic novels and the award-granting bodies that the graphic novel readers' advisor needs to watch and use as reference points are

Eisner (1988–), awarded annually at San Diego's Comic-Con International, provides recognition to stand-alone graphic novels as well as to issues in series. There are also annual awards for comic books, artists, and those who contribute to the technical sides of comics production, such as pencillers.

Glyph (2005–), awarded annually during the East Coast Black Age of Comics Convention, provides recognition to the best American comics made by, for, and about people of color. Interesting category awards include those for best self-published work and for best male and female characters.

Grand Prize of the City of Angoulême (1974–) honors a cartoonist for his or her body of work. The honoree may be French or foreign.

Harvey (1988–) has been awarded at a variety of American comics festivals and also includes division prizes specifically for writers, artists, and an array of formats including graphic novels.

Xeric Foundation funds comic book creators who are in the self-publishing stage of their career. To be awarded a Xeric identifies the recipient as a comics writer to watch, akin to authors who win MacArthur Genius Awards.

FAN SITES AND INSIGHTS

Not all fans are insightful, nor are all fan-built and/or fan-maintained websites appropriate readers' advisory tools. However, reading fan sites can acquaint the advisor with and update him or her in regard to the latest rising stars before more deliberate critics have gone to press to share trends. Reading fan sites also provides the advisor with vocabulary that can resonate with local readers searching for advice. Fan sites linked to well-known graphic novelists' own sites are especially likely to have some substantive content of their own.

A variety of media outlets provide blog postings and other published lists offered by graphic novel aficionados, especially toward the end of each calendar year. You can maintain dedicated links to some from previous years, as well as noting the current year's popularly acclaimed "bests." Among media to track for such nonspecialist suggestions are

All-TIME Graphic Novels (Arnold, Andrew. *Time*, 2005; www.time .com/time/2005/100books/0,24459,graphic_novels,00.html). While it's not yet certain that the dozen or so books on this list will stand a very long test of time, they are all appropriate choices for the advisor to have in her vocabulary when working with adult readers.

Collective: Comic and Graphic Novel Reviews and Features (BBC Two; www.bbc.co.uk/dna/collective/C1230/). While no longer actively maintained by the British broadcasting giant, this site offers an excellent complement of links to material on relatively recent, as well as classic, authors and titles in the graphic novel format. Contributors of the articles and commentaries include members of the public as well as BBC employees, creating a good mash-up of independent viewpoints.

Comics (*The Guardian*, Manchester, U.K.; www.guardian.co.uk/books/comics/). This link to one of England's best newspapers provides quick access to a wealth of advisory suggestions, including lists by American graphic novel expert Danny Fingeroth and features culled from sequential art news happening on the Continent.

National Public Radio offers regular coverage of all aspects of the book and reading world in interview and commentary broadcasts. Annual "best of" lists are available year-round on its website, including such annotated lists as "best Graphic Novels" (www.npr.org/templates/story/story.php?storyId=97636274).

PROFESSIONAL DEVELOPMENT COURSES AND CONFERENCE PROGRAMS

Seeking out and attending sessions on graphic novels and readers' advisory work is another venue to maintaining and building skill level. The Young Adult Library Services Association and other divisions of the American Library Association and state and regional library associations offer such programming on a regular basis. If you attend such a program and believe you aren't getting enough from it, then it may be time for you to design and offer such assistance to other advisors! Learning by teaching will sharpen your awareness of reader needs and applicable reader services.

Large cities throughout the United States host annual comics conventions that include instructive content as well as the opportunity to visit with creators, publishers, and fans. Three of the largest are held in New York City (www.nycomiccon.com), San Diego (www.comic-con.org/cci/), and the San Francisco Bay Area (www.comic-con.org/wc/). Conventions of this magnitude host year-round websites where you can find up-to-date information on this year's meeting dates and the program slate.

Even if you can't physically attend such a convention, be sure to look at content posted on the official websites. Each one sponsors awards, and knowledge of these winning artists and books is an obvious need of readers' advisors.

FINALLY

There is nothing final about providing reading advice. Reading this book should have prepared you to take your skills to a new level when connecting potential readers with graphic novels, but you'll need to practice and discover what else you can learn about both readers and the format. Keep reading graphic novels yourself, keep identifying potential readers, and keep learning about the nuances of the format.

Notes

1. D. Aviva Rothschild, *Graphic Novels: A Bibliographic Guide to Book-Length Comics* (Santa Barbara, CA: Libraries Unlimited, 1995).
2. Gene Kannenberg Jr., *500 Essential Graphic Novels: The Ultimate Guide* (New York: HarperCollins, 2008).
3. Danny Fingeroth, ed., *The Rough Guide to Graphic Novels* (London: Rough Guides Reference, 2008).
4. Michael Pawuk, *Graphic Novels: A Genre Guide to Comic Books, Manga, and More* (Santa Barbara, CA: Libraries Unlimited, 2006).
5. Art Spiegelman, *The Complete Maus* (New York: Pantheon, 1996).
6. Scott McCloud, *Understanding Comics: The Invisible Art* (New York: HarperPerennial, 1994); McCloud, *Making Comics: Storytelling Secrets of Comics, Manga and Graphic Novels* (New York: Harper, 2006).
7. McCloud, *Reinventing Comics: How Imagination and Technology Are Revolutionizing an Art Form* (New York: HarperPerennial, 2000).
8. Robin Varnum and Christina T. Gibbons, eds., *The Language of Comics: Word and Image* (Jackson: University Press of Mississippi, 2001).
9. Rocco Versaci, *This Book Contains Graphic Language: Comics as Literature* (London: Continuum, 2007).
10. Will Eisner, *Comics and Sequential Art* (Tamarac, FL: Poorhouse Press, 1985); Eisner, *Graphic Storytelling and Visual Narrative* (Tamarac, FL: Poorhouse Press, 1996); Chris Hart, *Drawing Crime Noir* (New York: Random House, Watson-Guptill, 2006); Hart, *Manga Mania* (New York: Random House, Watson-Guptill, 2001); Bob Pendarvis and Mark Kneece, *The Bristol Board Jungle* (New York: NBM, 2004).
11. Klaus Janson, *The DC Comics Guide to Pencilling Comics* (New York: Random House, Watson-Guptill, 2001).
12. Matt Madden, *99 Ways to Tell a Story* (New York: Chamberlain Brothers, 2005).
13. David S. Serchay, *The Librarian's Guide to Graphic Novels for Children and Tweens* (New York: Neal-Schuman, 2008).
14. Robin Brenner, *Understanding Manga and Anime* (Santa Barbara, CA: Libraries Unlimited, 2007); Stephen Cary, *Going Graphic: Comics at Work in the Multilingual Classroom* (Portsmouth, NH: Heinemann, 2004).

Appendix A

A SHORT COURSE FOR THE ADVISOR NEW TO GRAPHIC NOVELS

I f you as the readers' advisor, or members of your readers' advisory staff, lack a background in personal reading experience that includes a range of graphic novels, here is a crash course in what to read to get yourself up to the starting line. The titles listed here are presented in the order recommended for you to read, and the annotations include key concepts and questions to hold in mind as you approach each one. There are ten units, but the amount of reading suggested might take even the busiest staff member only about two weeks to achieve.

1. How does reading a graphic novel work?

Start with a title that requires you to attend to narrative flow, using both images and words to follow the story. I'd recommend Carol Lay's *The Big Skinny*, a nonfiction graphic novel about one woman' success in losing and keeping off weight, or James Sturm's *The Golem's Mighty Swing* (now collected in *James Sturm's America*), a piece of historical fiction from the segregated era of Negro and Jewish baseball leagues.[1] Each of these selections offers straightforward narrative, interesting characters, and information that may be of personal interest. The author and artist are a single individual in each of these cases, and the art is clear and accessible to most viewers.

As you read either of these, consider how the author moves you from concept to concept. How does she or he employ point of view in the images to communicate important information to you about events in the narrative? Spend time on a single page that has at least six panels and think about how you interpret what happens "off camera" as you move from the image in one panel to the image in the next. Are you able to pin down your own insertion of movement on the static page?

2. How do different styles of art fit different narratives in terms of content, mood, and theme?

Move on to an anthology that offers you same-book access to a relatively large number of creators working on a similar topic or theme. Among good options for this are the collection *Postcards: True Stories That Never Happened*, edited by Jason Rodriguez, or a volume from editor Tom Pomplun's Graphic Classics series, such as *Twain, Jack London,* or *Gothic Classics.*[2] Either of these options provides you with a relatively small volume that brings together more than a dozen different pieces.

As you read one of these, be generous with the time you take to flip back and forth to compare and contrast visual rendering styles, including techniques and moods evoked in the viewer. Do you find yourself attracted to, or wanting to take more time with, a particular visual style? By the time you have read the volume in its entirety, can you identify which parts of it attracted you more than others? Which parts put you off and why?

3. What's it like to give up text altogether and read a book that is composed entirely of images?

Especially if you find yourself prone to skipping over visual content, or resistant to incorporating the reading of it into your attempts to understand how reading a graphic novel works, you may need to take this remedial break. I'd suggest you stick with a wordless book written for adult readers, rather than for children, because you are an adult reader and the point here is to tap the sophisticated reading experiences you already possess. If you are undertaking this "short course" on your own, you may want to find some reviews of the wordless book you select *after* you've read it, and see how your understanding squares with those of readers experienced in visual literacy. If you can, then have some coworkers read the same title you chose and discuss it.

For this endeavor, I'd suggest you read either Andy Hartzell's *Fox Bunny Funny,* which, although disguised as a cute animal story, is actually a story about owning and asserting one's identity in the face of others' preconceptions, or Shinsuke Tanaka's *Wings,* an all-ages story about friendship across a brief lifespan.[3]

As you read either (or both) of these wordless books, what do you notice about the need to take the pages in order? What kinds of complexity seem to be present—that of ideas, emotions, narrative design? Do you ever become lost from the narrative thread? And if you do, how do you find your way again?

4. What's it like to take on a longer narrative and use your new skills with a book that may take multiple sittings to read through completely?

Just as new readers of traditional texts move from books that can be completed in a single sitting to ones that require the ability to pause and then pick up where you stopped reading, you may need to practice reconnecting with the narrative thread of a graphic novel that you have put aside. For this exercise, I recommend that you choose a title that you know will be too long for you to complete in one or even two sittings. The point here is to consider how you carry what you've read across time (however brief) to the next point when you take up the same book. Depending on your personal genre tastes and the development of your graphic novel reading ease, you may want to try Kia Asamiya's *Batman: Child of Dreams*, from a superhero universe—or you may prefer the fairy tale riff to be found in the complete first volume of Linda Medley's *Castle Waiting*.[4]

Your reading of either of these books, for this exercise, includes the time you aren't reading; that is, a consideration of how you bridge the time gap that occurs in your approaching the full narrative. Do you find that you are able to pick up the book where you left off in the same way—whatever that way is—as you do a traditional print text? At what points in the reading do you break? Does the creator offer you suggested breaking points, and are these useful to you?

5. Explore the use of sequential art as part of a narrative that also utilizes other formats in the telling of a single story.

Sequential art may be part of a larger portfolio of presentation styles used by some authors to convey one connected narrative. Reading such works helps you to more fully grasp how sequential art provides both information and mood in contrast to and comparison with other formats. Try *The Magical Life of Long Tack Sam*, Ann Marie Fleming's biography of her ancestor, a man who lived the global life generations ahead of today's technology-enhanced capacities to network internationally, or Lucy Knisley's travel diary *French Milk*.[5]

How does the use of sequential art enhance the mood of the narrative? How is the sequential art approach sustained or expanded by other media used to recount the narrative? Would you prefer to read the same story in a different format? Would its presentation in a different format render the narrative into a different story in terms of information available to the reader, flow, or theme?

6. You've heard lots about manga, but have you tried it on for size?

Because manga has become so popular as a library collection choice selected for American teens, some adults new to graphic novels are particularly resistant to sampling its aesthetics for themselves. And because of assertive marketing, it's important that the readers' advisor have a good feel for what makes manga both the same as and different from other graphic novel options. Manga and its cognates are now available from several countries other than Japan. And Japanese culture informs Japanese comics quite specifically. For this portion of your crash course then, you'll consider two titles, one a Japanese import that's been translated and the other manga produced in the West.

One of the perceived barriers to reading modern translations of Japanese manga is the editorial decision made by many translators in the past five or more years to present English text without "translating" the layout to conform to Western left-to-right reading standards. If you haven't tried reading a layout from right to left, this may make you feel anxious. That's fine, but try it anyway!

If you are feeling industrious, you might try one of the annual volumes of *The Mammoth Book of Best New Manga,* an anthology edited by Ilya that will offer you dozens of short manga pieces in one place.[6] If you are willing to try reading a book from right to left and want a manageable first effort, pick up the first volume of Natsuki Takaya's popular romantic comedy Fruits Basket, but be sure it's the "unflipped" version (a language translation that maintains the panels and pages in Japanese order).[7]

To get a firmer grasp on how manga, as a style, transcends country or culture of origin, try a Western title that utilizes the aesthetic genre. You might try Russian Canadian Svetlana Chmakova's *Nightschool,* a tale of discreet vampires, or the nonfiction biography *The 14th Dalai Lama* by Tetsu Saiwai.[8]

Keep in mind that manga comprises a rich and varied array of genres, both stylistic and in terms of content. Your introduction to its array is intended to be only a first dip, the opportunity to get your advisor's toe into the ocean of possibilities!

7. What does a major award-winning graphic novel look like and read like?

Specific awards for graphic novels and their creators are discussed in this book. You'll want to sample some of these wares to provide yourself with what experts judge as quality in the format. Choose something from one of the awards listed in chapter 2, or pick up Printz winner and National Book Award short list–holder Gene Luen Yang's *American Born Chinese*, which weaves together three narrative strands into one compelling and literary novel, or Angoulême-honored creator Lewis Trondheim's *Little Nothings*, a collection of insightful and wry autobiographical admissions.[9]

How does either of these titles compare to and contrast with other graphic novels you have read so far in this mini-course? Which specific attributes strike you as stellar? How would you compare one of these two titles to other literary award-winners like Pulitzer-winning Harper Lee's *To Kill a Mockingbird*, or cinema winners like the Oscar-winning *Crash*? What aspects do exemplary graphic novels perhaps share with exemplary print literature? With film? With visual art?

8. Can a graphic novel give you information that standard news sources can't?

Nonfiction sequential art, at its best, can provide the reader with a different perspective than can a newspaper, website, or newsreel. I'd suggest you explore Joe Sacco's *Safe Area Gorazde*, a trained cartoon journalist's account of aspects of the Bosnian war of the early 1990s, or a volume from Rick Geary's series A Treasury of Victorian Murder.[10]

How does the graphic novelist use point of view? How does his accuracy compare to and contrast with narrative accounts you have read of the event? What did you learn here that had escaped your understanding of the topic when you learned about it in previously read or viewed accounts? What's missing from the graphic novel that you believe is essential to understanding the topic?

9. Choose a tool from chapter 8 and select two more graphic novels from it for yourself, based on the book or website's description.

Did you make your selection based on name recognition? Or were you driven by genre interests? Or interest in any art that was included in the recommendation? Think about how you made the choices, and, after you read each of the books you selected for yourself, how well the advice that brought you to choose them represented your reading experience with them.

10. As you do with any other area of literature for which you are responsible as an advisor, don't stop reading.

Read new graphic novels, but also remember to go back and read ones that were published years ago and that have become part of the canon of "gn classics." A readers' advisor's preparation for the job is always under way, and that is no less true for the graphic novel readers' advisor than for any other.

Notes

1. Carol Lay, *The Big Skinny: How I Changed My Fattitude* (New York: Villard, 2008), is a memoir offering sound advice on how to lose weight by counting calories and adding exercise to the daily regimen. James Sturm, *The Golem's Mighty Swing* (Montreal: Drawn and Quarterly, 2001), provides a fictional but historically accurate take on the era in American baseball when major leagues were segregated and players of color barnstormed to earn a meager living.
2. Jason Rodriguez, ed., *Postcards: True Stories That Never Happened* (New York: Villard, 2007), includes short stories by a variety of current American cartoonists and graphic novelists, each springing from a unique message-bearing antique postcard purchased at a flea market or yard sale. Tom Pomplun's series of Graphic Classics (Mount Horeb, WI: Eureka Productions) has been published for about a decade. Each volume treats the major, and some minor, works by canonical literary authors, by presenting interpretations of his or her short stories, poems, and even novels by any of about a dozen graphic novelists who contribute to each volume.
3. Andy Hartzell, *Fox Bunny Funny* (Marietta, GA: Top Shelf Productions, 2007); Shinsuke Tanaka, *Wings* (Port Washington, NY: Purple Bear Books, 2006).
4. Kia Asamiya's *Batman: Child of Dreams* (New York: DC Comics, 2003) doesn't give you the best known of the covey of Batman artists and writers, but the story and storyboarding are compelling and accessible, whether you know the Batman legend or not. Linda Medley's *Castle Waiting* (Seattle: Fantagraphics, 2006) is the first collection of this continuing fractured fairy tale, offering a complement of story arcs and sufficient closure to make reading satisfying.
5. Ann Marie Fleming's *The Magical Life of Long Tack Sam* (New York: Riverhead Books, 2007) is presented through drawn panel art, photography, documents, and other visual and text means, highly appropriate to memorializing the life of a peripatetic magician who ensured that his descendants were multicultural. Lucy Knisley's *French Milk* (New York: Simon and Schuster, 2008) recounts the creator's trip to Paris with her mother and how, at the age of twenty-two, she recognized the maturation of her own worldview.
6. Start with the latest edition of *The Mammoth Book of Best New Manga*, edited by Ilya and published annually since 2006 by Running Press. Each edition offers not only dozens of short but complete manga, but also concise commentary on the different styles represented by the pieces.

7. Fruits Basket by Natsuki Takaya (Los Angeles: TokyoPop, 2004–) is, like many Japanese imports of manga to be marketed in mainstream American retailing channels, a long and still ongoing series. Elements of manga incorporated into this particular volume are edifying: the representation of expressions; plot details that include mystery, romance, and fantasy; and characterizations that treat social classes as well as personality clashes with humor.

8. Svetlana Chmakova's *Nightschool* (New York: Yen Press, 2009–) begins a new series that will be completed in the next few years. *The 14th Dalai Lama* by Tetsu Saiwai (Los Angeles: Emotional Content, 2008) offers a biography of this Nobel Peace Prize winner from his childhood education for leadership through the ongoing war between Tibet and China, and into his current age of retrospection.

9. Gene Luen Yang, *American Born Chinese* (New York: First Second Books, 2006); Lewis Trondheim, *Little Nothings: The Curse of the Umbrella* (New York: NBM, ComicsLit, 2008). Both of these writers utilize autobiographical material and fantasy, work in full color, and offer voices and perspectives that don't fit neatly into any genre niche.

10. Joe Sacco, *Safe Area Gorazde: The War in Eastern Bosnia, 1992–1995* (Seattle: Fantagraphics, 2000). This is a fine example of cartoon journalism, in which the author holds a university degree. Rick Geary, A Treasury of Victorian Murder (New York: NBM, ComicsLit, 1987–), includes nine volumes and may continue to grow. Each volume presents factual information, in text and image, of a historic murder case, many of which have not been satisfactorily solved even a century or more later.

Appendix B

BASIC MANGA TERMS

The traditions surrounding Japanese manga, for both creators and publishers and for American readers, are steep. Presently, manga holds high rank among a segment of comics readers and so the graphic novel readers' advisor should have some knowledge of how and where the areas of manga-specific and broader graphic novel and comics reading pleasure intersect, as well as where the technical differences between manga and non-manga graphic novels comics lie. This is best done through one's own deep sampling as well as by reading books such as Robin Brenner's *Understanding Manga and Anime,* referenced in chapter 8, or learning from the many websites devoted to manga and manga publishing.

Listed here are some basic terms to help you understand reviews and other references in manga reference sources. This is not an exhaustive glossary, but a brief overview to help you on your way if you pursue this related area of comics and advising.

PRESUMED AUDIENCES

Ecchi. Contains story lines and images that are sexualized but not decidedly adult in content, in juxtaposition to . . .

Hentai. Explicitly sexual content appropriate to an adult audience that expects and wants such material.

Josei. Manga oriented to older women readers, often thematizing romance and family or work issues.

Kodomo. Manga created for and oriented to readers who are children, containing themes and images appropriate to preadolescents.

Seinen. Manga targeting adult male readers in both coming-of-age story concepts and imagery thematizing the strength and issues of an individual.

Shojo. Manga targeting teenage girls in both character-driven concept and imagery, and marketing.

Shonen. Manga targeting teenage boys with action and sometimes fantasy themes.

Steampunk. Genre of speculative fiction represented in manga but also in text-only works, consisting of Victorian Era settings melded with science fiction machinery.

Yaoi. Manga depicting romantic and sometimes explicitly sexual male/male relationships, targeting female as well as fewer male readers.

Yuri. Manga thematizing female/female relationships, sometimes sexualized or romantic.

PROVENANCES

Dojinshi. Independently published manga, as distinct from that which is produced in established manga houses.

Manhwa. Manga from Korea, which is read left to right.

Tankobon. Story published complete in a single volume, in distinction from the multivolume publishing more typical of manga stories available to American readers.

For an interesting essay on approaching the unique aesthetic of manga, see cultural anthropologist Matt Thorn's "The Face of the Other" (www.matt-thorn.com/mangagaku/faceoftheother.html).

INDEX

Authors, titles, subjects, and series are interfiled in one alphabet. Authors and series are printed in roman, titles in italic, and subjects in boldface. References to notes are indicated by *n* following the page number (e.g., 111n8); references to tables are indicated by *t*.

A

Abel, Jessica, 59, 65

Abouet, Marguerite, 21, 63

adaptations from text to sequential art, 85–88

adolescent and teen readers, 2, 28–29, 43

adult readers, 29, 32–33

Adventures in Oz, 87

The Adventures of Captain Underpants series, 28

The Adventures of Tintin series, 4, 21, 88–89

aesthetics, 20

After 9/11: America's War on Terrorism, 2001–, 86

Age of Bronze series, 41, 80

age of readers, 19

Alan's War: The Memories of G. I. Alan Cope, 72

Alice in Sunderland, 93–94

All Movie Guide (website), 50

All-TIME Graphic Novels (website), 102

American Born Chinese, viii, 80, 109, 111n9

American Splendor (film), 17n13

Anderson, Ho Che, 22, 74

Angoulême, Grand Prize of the City of, 101

An Anthology of Graphic Fiction, Cartoons, and True Stories, 90

appeal factors

complexity, 26

formats, 82–83

generally, 5–7

image/text balance, 23–24

layout, 23

point of view, 27

from RUSA/CODES Readers' Advisory Committee, 12–13

supporting work, 24

visual style, 21–23

Appollodorus, Olivier, 40, 64

Arnold, Andrew, 102

The Arrival, 84

Art School Confidential (film version of *Eightball*), 50

As the World Burns, 75

Asamiya, Kia, 107, 110n4

Asayuki, Umeka, 80

Asterix series, 14, 88

auditory preferences of readers, 6, 24

Auster, Paul, 85

awards

examples, 101–102

and promotion of books, 13, 16

in training, 109

Awkward and Definition, 73

Aya, 21, 63

Aya of Yop City, 63

Ayroles, Françoise, 86

Azaceta, Paul, 70

You may also be interested in

The Readers' Advisory Guide to Genre Fiction, Second Edition: Provocative and spirited, this guide offers hands-on strategies for librarians who want to become experts at figuring out what their readers are seeking and how to match books with those interests.

Serving Teens through Readers' Advisory: Filled with concrete advice, this guide supports public librarians as well as middle and high school library media specialists and library support staff who want to make an impact on teens at a critical time in their lives.

The Readers' Advisory Guide to Nonfiction: This hands-on guide includes nonfiction bibliography, key authors, benchmark books with annotations, and core collections. It is useful for readers' advisory and collection development, helping librarians, library workers, and patrons select great reading from the entire library collection!

Graphic Novels Now: By focusing on monographic works in a practical, in-depth professional discussion, this guide helps librarians grapple with the details of a growing genre and customer base that rarely fit into an easy model.

Check out these and other great titles at www.alastore.ala.org!